The Texas Jury Rules

By James M. Stanton and Trey Cox

Printed in the United States of America.

Copyright © 2011 by James M. Stanton and Trey Cox. Dallas, TX.

ISBN: 978-0-615-52235-7

This book is dedicated to trial court judges and jurors who, by their oath and willingness to serve, are the workhorses of the federal and state judiciary in Texas. You make us proud to be trial lawyers.

Table of Contents

Foreword

Juries matter. Juries matter a lot. They are the imperative institution of democracy in America's judicial system. Yet, jury trials are diminishing and the trend has disturbing consequences for the future of our nation's jurisprudence. For one thing, since there are fewer jury trials, fewer lawyers know how to try jury cases. Because of this fact, *The Texas Jury Rules* by James Stanton and Trey Cox is an important book, thoughtfully illustrating for trial lawyers what is important to jurors, in the actual words of people who have served as jurors in Texas courts.

The book's methodology to determine juror attitudes is creative. While he was sitting as a trial judge, James Stanton invited people who had been jurors in his court to return for videotaped interviews. Along with Trey Cox, James then synthesized the results into a fascinating montage of vignettes that instruct and enlighten. Anyone who wants to be effective before a jury will profit greatly from this book.

Yet, it is not only lawyers (and judges for that matter) who can profit from this book. Everyone can, because it illustrates how conscientious and diligent our citizens are when they sit on juries. Indeed, cynicism toward juries is wrong-headed, because juries do as good a job in performing their duties as is humanly possible. They are not perfect, but they get very close. And without juries, our justice system would be a far different and a much less American institution. As one observer aptly noted, "Adherence to, and execution of, the law is dependent upon the buy in of the citizenry and the social capital created through public participation in legal institutions. Lose that, and we might lose it all."

James Stanton and Trey Cox are doing their part to exalt the jury and to improve jury trials. For their most excellent contribution, we are in their debt.

W. Royal Furgeson, Jr.
Senior U.S. District Judge
Northern District of Texas

Introduction
By James M. Stanton

During my time on the bench, I welcomed every jury to my courtroom with these remarks.

"Ladies and gentlemen: You live in the greatest country the world has ever known. You are privileged to be citizens of the single greatest society in all of human history. There has never been another country like the United States of America—ever. You should know that one of the many reasons for our nation's greatness is that we have a robust right to trial by jury enshrined in the Seventh Amendment. The Seventh Amendment is effective only when everyday citizens accept the invitation that arrives in their mailboxes in the form of a jury summons asking them to serve their communities.

The parties before you in court today have exercised their Constitutional right to have a jury of their peers decide the disputed facts in this case. For this reason I have summoned you to my courtroom. On behalf of the citizens of Dallas County and the State of Texas, let me be among the first to thank you for answering the call for jury duty."

From there, each trial took its own course as the jury was selected, the lawyers gave opening statements, and the jurors dutifully considered the testimony and evidence in cases involving everything from breach of contract and securities fraud all the way to employment discrimination, wrongful death, and motor vehicle accidents. After the evidence closed, I would read the jury charge, the lawyers would give their closing arguments, and the bailiff would hand the jury the verdict form and evidence. The jury would retire to the jury room for their deliberations where the real final argument— the one among the jurors—took place.

For those of us left in the courtroom, the waiting would begin. The lawyers, their clients, courtroom observers, and the court staff all wondered: Who will be the foreperson? What do the jurors think about this witness or that piece of evidence? What did they think of the lawyers? What evidence did they find most persuasive? What are they going to decide? How long will it take? The idea for this project, *The Texas Jury Rules*, came from those hours of waiting and wondering. This book sets out to answer these, and other, vital questions about what is really important to jurors, based on videotaped, post-trial interviews.

In Texas, state trial court judges must instruct their jurors that they may not talk about the case—even with their spouses—until the verdict is returned. The jurors are further instructed that they may not talk about the case even with their fellow jurors until they have heard all the evidence and begin their deliberations. I encouraged my juries to strictly follow these instructions by offering to come into the jury room after they returned their verdicts to answer any questions they had. My juries would sit and talk to me, sometimes for hours, about their experience. The genesis of this book is the raw and powerful feedback I received from jurors during those conversations.

Upon retiring to the jury room following a verdict, I would take off my robe and sit at the end of the table and simply ask, "What do you think?" The most common first question from the jurors was "Did we get it right?" My response always encompassed two principles: first, their decision was correct because it reflected the collective decision of twelve qualified persons; and second, their decision was one of many legally acceptable answers to the questions in the jury charge. I would tell them to be proud of their service and their decision.

From there, my conversations with my jurors varied widely, but common themes developed regarding their experience. I would even go so far as to say that I could see a set of basic rules developing from the juror comments. Even as the lawyers, witnesses, and facts of each case changed, the feedback from jurors was remarkably consistent. As I tried more cases, I witnessed trial lawyers—even some very experienced trial lawyers—running afoul of these basic rules, and I began to realize there would be a great deal of value in capturing these sentiments and sharing them with trial practitioners everywhere. But what was I going to do, ask the jurors to quit their jobs and go on the lecture circuit with me to teach trial lawyers how to relate to jurors? Then one of my interns suggested that we videotape a few juror interviews and use them as a teaching tool. So I began asking jurors to sit for videotaped interviews. Rather than personally conducting the interviews, I had my law student interns do them. I spent several hours with them, composing a list of common questions and issues to explore with each juror. It was a great learning experience for them and yielded a treasure trove of information for practicing lawyers.

The videotaped interviews were collected during 2009 and 2010 from jurors who served in civil cases before the 134th Judicial District Court in Dallas County, Texas. The district courts are the highest level trial courts in the Texas judicial system; consequently, the cases these jurors considered included significant damage claims. I committed to keep their identities anonymous (of course, I told them I could not prevent someone from recognizing them when their videotaped interview was shown) and asked that they not identify lawyers, parties, and witnesses by name. Finally, I promised the jurors I would use their interviews to make presentations to other lawyers, judges, and citizens about the importance of the right to trial by jury.

Hundreds of jurors shared their thoughts, and over 60 agreed to sit for videotaped interviews resulting in over 25 hours of footage. The interviews ranged in length from 10 minutes to over an hour. Initially, the jurors were asked open-ended questions with more direct follow-up questions. No subject was off limits. By having my interns conduct the interviews, I believe we received open and unvarnished answers to many of our questions. Reviewing the interviews was a powerful experience because the jurors shared their most intimate thoughts about the trials in which they served. They explained how they picked their foreperson, how they conducted their deliberations, what witnesses and evidence they found persuasive, what they thought about the lawyers, how proud they were to serve as jurors, and how to make the whole process better.

The project turned out far better than I imagined possible, and I quickly acknowledged the responsibility to share this information with others. I also realized that it would be a substantial undertaking to review 25 hours of interview footage, analyze the data, and organize it for effective presentation. I decided I needed a partner for this project, someone who had actual jury trial experience, a passion for courtroom psychology, and boundless energy. In sum, I needed someone to help me in my stewardship of the collective knowledge entrusted to me by my jurors. I needed my friend, Trey Cox!

Trey Cox is the most effective communicator I have ever met. He is a board-certified civil trial lawyer at Texas' premier commercial litigation boutique. Trey has successfully tried dozens of high-stakes business cases to verdict and received numerous professional acknowledgments, but these successes are just a byproduct of his passion for excellence in the courtroom. His writing and presentations on courtroom decision-making and the effective use of demonstrative evidence have changed the way lawyers communicate with judges and juries.

Over lunch in September 2010, I thankfully welcomed Trey as a partner on this project. During the next year we analyzed the 25 hours of interview footage. Initially, we plucked out over 300 clips to use in making presentations for judges, lawyers, and law students. We had the privilege of presenting the juror videos to the Garland Walker Inn of Court in Houston, the Texas College for Newly-Appointed and Elected Judges in Austin, the Trial Skills Section of the Dallas Bar Association, and the annual meeting of the Texas Trial Lawyers Association. These initial presentations focused on jurors' opinions about different aspects of trial advocacy. The response was overwhelmingly positive. We found there was a tremendous appetite for the information we were sharing. People wanted more. They asked for rules; they asked for checklists. They asked for something they could have as a takeaway that contained the lessons and rules of the juror interviews. This book, *The Texas Jury Rules*, is our response to those requests.

In this book, we have taken what the jurors said in their interviews and distilled ten specific rules. Each rule contains some of the best quotations from the juror interviews about that specific aspect of trial presentation. Of course, each rule will give rise to a few war stories along with some of our opinions. Many of the opinions offered by the jurors are common sense; nonetheless they are lessons that deserve repeating. Some of the opinions—and maybe some of the rules—will surprise you. They may even be contrary to the conventional wisdom of so-called experts of jury trial advocacy. Keep in mind however, that we support each of the rules with the words of Texas jurors.

We hope that you will find these rules valuable to your trial practice. The right to trial by jury is one of the crown jewels of American society. We owe it to our clients and the judges and juries who serve in our judicial system to present our client's best case.

We appreciate your support and the fact that you purchased this book. We want to hear from you if you have comments. There are several ways you can do so. First we have a website dedicated to this project and the book: TheTexasJuryRules.com. We will from time to time provide new information and content as well as notice of our speaking engagements. In addition, you can reach me at JamesMStanton@andrewskurth.com or Trey at tcox@lynnllp.com. Like you, we have active trial practices and busy personal and professional lives, but we are committed to responding to everyone. We hope you enjoy the book and look forward to hearing from you.

James M. Stanton
September 2011

Rules Summary

Following is a summary chapter that holds the lessons you will learn from the jurors throughout the book. As you prepare for trial, we hope you will use this summary to help you quickly revisit the primary tenets of *The Texas Jury Rules*. Of course, we encourage you to read each chapter carefully and pay special attention to the words of the jurors.

The Texas Jury Rules: Attitude

Rule 1: Respect the Process

Courtrooms are located in government buildings with wood paneling, presided over by a judge who sits in an elevated throne-like position above the jurors, lawyers, observers, and parties in dispute. The courtroom is a solemn place where serious issues are resolved. In nearly every interview we conducted, one thing that came through was the importance jurors placed on his or her surroundings. The aura of the courtroom caused them to feel that what they were doing was important. One juror compared his experience to being in church. For those of us who spend our days in court, it is our job to maintain that solemn environment. That means showing the proper level of respect for the process and the players. No matter how much we think that a thundering "you can't handle the truth" moment is a good examination, jurors expect something different. They expect you to be respectful. This means treating the jury, the courtroom staff, and witnesses with respect and dignity—at all times.

Rule 2: Be Prepared

Jurors expect you to have mastered your facts and evidence before trial. They expect you to know the law, rules of evidence, and the judge's preferences, too. From the jury's perspective, what does it mean for a lawyer to be prepared? As one juror told us, he expects the lawyers to "know what they are going to do before they do it." If you wait to prepare until you arrive at the courthouse, the jury will know it. Jurors told us that they expect lawyers to "only ask the questions that matter" and "get to the point." When using technology or playing videotaped depositions, the jurors tell us they don't want lawyers to "stumble over admitting exhibits" or "fumble around;" instead, they expect things to be "cued up and ready to go." As described fully in this chapter, the best method to ensure that you do not run afoul of the jury's expectations is tireless preparation before you enter the courthouse.

The Texas Jury Rules: Effective Trial Presentation

Rule 3: Be Credible

The jurors told us that the most important attribute of an attorney or witness is credibility. They describe in vivid detail why they trusted some lawyers and witnesses and why others were considered untrustworthy. Even though jurors do not spend their days in courtrooms or possess law degrees, they are masters in the art of judging people. That is why we have this process in the first place. Like you and me, they size people up every day and decide who is trustworthy and credible. Their life experiences qualify them as credibility experts: they raise children, they deal with office politics, and they navigate the in-laws visiting for the holidays. They know when someone is manipulating them or telling half of the truth. Our analysis of the interviews established that, in each case, the jury is looking for a guide. The guide is the person who will lead them through the forest of witnesses, documents, and trial procedures to help them find their way. If you can become their trusted guide, they are likely to follow you home—to a favorable verdict for your client.

Rule 4: Set Expectations

Most jurors don't know what to expect when they appear for jury duty. During their interviews, we heard them wonder, "How will this affect my life?" and "How long will it take to finish the trial?" They worry about how their bosses will react to taking time off for jury duty ("Can I be fired?") and whether they can fulfill the promise to attend a daughter's soccer game by 6 p.m. on Thursday. If the judge does not provide guidance about the length of the trial, it becomes the responsibility of the lawyer during voir dire. Your jurors are a blank slate with respect to courtroom processes so take advantage of your tabula rasa to teach them. You will start to earn their trust and gain credibility. One juror aptly told us that her experience was "nothing like it appears on T.V." After all, as the jurors told us, they wanted the lawyers to tell them how many witnesses would be called to testify, how long each will be on the witness stand, and why the testimony and other evidence being presented was important. Immediately before closing argument, when the jury charge and verdict form are read, jurors find out what is important to the judge. Jurors told us that after reading the questions they were supposed to answer in the jury charge, they were surprised by how the lawyers had spent their time during the trial. Jurors told us they want lawyers to more carefully structure their cases around the questions in the jury charge. When you accurately set expectations for the jury, you become a person of influence, a good role to have when the jurors' final decision—the answers to the questions in the jury charge—is being made.

Rule 5: Be Sincere

In this chapter we analyze what strategies and tactics the passionate advocate can use to capitalize on the jury's desire to do justice. Jurors told us they respect, and even admire, lawyers who advocate zealously for their clients. A juror bemoaned one lawyer for just "going through the motions" and thought that the lawyer "shouldn't represent the client if [he didn't] believe in the case." Another juror wanted to know she was "doing the right thing" by her verdict. What do jurors think of crying? What about the personal injury plaintiff claiming back injuries who wore three-inch heels every day of the trial? Conversely, jurors also describe how unpersuasive purely emotional arguments are.

Rule 6: Be Transparent

Jurors repeatedly told us that they believed some lawyers and witnesses were trying to hide the truth. In Texas, state trial court judges instruct the jury that they must consider all the evidence admitted in the case, but the jury decides how the evidence is to be weighed. Being transparent means understanding that to the jury there is one case that has all the evidence. The jury doesn't separate plaintiff's facts and defendant's facts; jurors don't care whether the plaintiff or defendant offered an exhibit or called a witness to the stand. But something they will not forget is who objects; and as they told us, they will not forget who tries to hide information from them. In this chapter, jurors teach us that there is a difference between making every possible objection in order to get an "A" on a law school evidence examination and making the right objections in a courtroom. In their interviews, jurors recount how successful evidence objections affected the lawyer's credibility and the client's case during their deliberations as they wondered out loud: "What was he trying to hide from us?" or "Why can't we listen to the whole conversation on the tape?" or "Why were those documents redacted?" Jurors expect the lawyers to be responsible for all the facts. When we aren't, jurors think the lawyer "must have something to hide." Experienced trial lawyers know that every case that goes to trial has good and bad facts for each side. Great trial lawyers know how to account for the bad facts and explain to the jury why they do not matter or how the conclusion being urged remains the right conclusion, despite some bad facts.

The Texas Jury Rules: Putting on Your Evidence

Rule 7: Get to the Point

Like you and me, jurors have spouses, kids, jobs, and lives they want to get back to. They willingly give their time in jury service, but it is our job to make good use of it. We have to ensure that we demonstrate through our words and deeds that we appreciate and value the time jurors are giving to help our clients resolve their differences. How do we show jurors that we are making efficient use of their valuable time? Jurors tell us they appreciate it when "all of a lawyer's questions seem to matter" and do not like it when "lawyers just kept droning on" until they can find the right documents. They also do not like waiting while lawyers look for documents, struggle with technology, or try to decide what witness to call next. One juror asked, "If you've had this case for five years, how do you not know everything about it already?" Another pet peeve of jurors is when they keep hearing the same thing "over and over and over." It makes them wonder, "Do you not think we heard you the first time, or the second time, or the third time?" In this chapter jurors describe ways that lawyers creatively communicated important information and the positive effect it had on their decision-making process.

Rule 8: Stay Focused

The trial lawyer's singular goal in the courtroom is to effectively communicate the facts, themes, and conclusions in a clear and memorable way. Anything that distracts from this goal hurts our client's case. Jurors described how lawyers' mannerisms, nervous ticks, and bad habits distract them. In this chapter we analyze the danger of a distracted jury. Jurors described how they had competitions to decide how long an attorney would drag out the "o" in "so" before each question on cross examination; or in another trial, they counted how many times an attorney twisted his eyebrow each day. One juror lamented the use of "air quotes" which, in his opinion, showed bad manners; and regardless of what Miss Manners would say, it caused jurors to fixate on "coming out of the jury box if we could to tie his hands to his sides!" These stories are humorous unless you are the lawyer with the distracting habit—or worse—the client whose lawyer is distracting the jury from your best arguments. Ask yourself this question: is the jury counting how many times you twist your eyebrows? Is the jury plotting to tie your hands to your sides? If yes, what is the likelihood that the jurors are paying attention to the substance of your client's case?

Rule 9: Use PowerPoint Slides and Demonstratives Effectively

Jurors tell us that effectively using demonstrative evidence is a powerful trial skill. Entire books have been written on effectively using PowerPoint slides. Graphic design firms have been established solely to assist lawyers in creating demonstrative evidence at trial. One juror described how a demonstrative exhibit showed how "tragic" an accident was and "helped her see clearly how everything happened." Another juror, who was an actress, provided a detailed analysis of how demonstrative evidence should have been used in her case but wasn't. Too often lawyers present confusing graphics or slides with twelve bullet points and a page worth of words. Neuroscience teaches us that loading slides with too much information causes a phenomenon we call "juror overload." In this chapter we explore describing how lawyers effectively use demonstrative evidence to enhance their trial presentations and to ensure that jurors understand and remember the key points of their clients' cases.

Rule 10: Present Credible Witnesses

It is hard to over-emphasize the importance of choosing the right witnesses and preparing those witnesses to tell your client's story. Recognizing this, it is now common for jury consultants to offer "witness school" for problem witnesses. Witnesses actually attend classes and preparation sessions where they learn how to answer questions in a way that makes them look truthful. In the jury's eyes, the lawyer is the chief spokesperson for the client. While they look to the lawyer to be the guide, they also remember that the judge has instructed them that what the lawyers say is not evidence. Instead, the jurors are told to consider the evidence admitted during the course of the trial. For this reason, who you choose to testify and how each witness presents to the jury are the foundation for your case. When a lawyer's arguments are not backed up by credible testimony from witnesses, jurors describe the effect on their decision-making process. One complained about her difficulty in judging the credibility of a witness who was presented by reading a written deposition (rather than offering videotaped deposition testimony or live testimony) because "ninety percent of what the person is saying is how they are saying it." In this chapter, the jurors provide a detailed description of what makes a credible witness.

Rule 1:
Respect The Process

People responding to the call for jury duty have expectations about the trial process. The Seventh Amendment right to a jury trial is unique to America; and as a nation, we have come to believe we are entitled to it. Collectively, we acknowledge the necessity of jury duty; and American school children are taught the importance of the right to trial by jury and this popular quote by one of our founding fathers, Thomas Jefferson: "I consider trial by jury as the only anchor ever yet imagined by man, by which a government can be held to the principles of its constitution."

In this chapter the jurors describe their expectation that lawyers and parties should treat the jury trial process with respect. Specifically, jurors tell us what behaviors and vocabulary communicate to them that we understand and respect the process. In addition to our overall attitude, the jurors outline specific expectations for how we should interact with them, the judge, his staff, opposing counsel, and the witnesses.

• *Recognize the Jurors' Sense of Duty*

Although jurors may groan about jury duty and many would prefer to be practically anywhere else, nevertheless most jurors are anything but apathetic about their role in the trial. Once selected to serve on a panel, jurors feel a great sense of civic duty. They recognize the seriousness of the dispute and the importance of their part in the trial proceeding. Because jurors are responsible for the outcome reached during deliberations, they strive to reach the right result. Several jurors have told us that they revere the courtroom and the role they play in the justice system. One juror compared witnessing a trial to attending church.

"I think the aura of the courtroom itself and the aura of the process that takes place within that courtroom is a very important factor in ensuring that the jury takes everything very seriously. I made an analogy before that it's kind of like going to church. The minute you're walking into church, you're sort of in that different frame of mind. And I think it's worth spending the money as a governmental jurisdiction to have a courtroom that looks very dignified, has the wood paneling, has the judge up on the bench wearing a robe—just to ensure that everybody treats the whole process with the respect that it should be treated."

Whether it be a church or synagogue, we sit quietly and reverently out of respect for the worship service. Not to be sacreligious, but in a similar way, silence and respect are an important part of the judicial process that must be honored. Even if they have never spent a moment in a courtroom, jurors instinctively expect a more formal vocabulary; they expect lawyers to stand when speaking and to wait for permission from the judge before proceeding. Attorneys know that trials are very serious and must work to make sure their actions are in accordance with this solemn environment. Jurors can too easily interpret an attorney's blithe or flippant behavior in the courtroom as a sign of disrespect.

Are we saying you should never use humor or modify your voice to make a point? No. But what we are saying is that you have to carefully monitor your behavior before a jury. We have and do use humor before juries, but it is better to wait and gauge the jurors before going in that direction. If you are unsure about whether humor or sarcasm is appropriate, it probably is best to pass. For those of us who spend our days in courtrooms, we can become too familiar with the process; and our familiarity can be misunderstood as a lack of respect.

• *Participate in the Necessary Formalities*

Although many trial formalities and procedures interfere with clear communication with the jury, some formality genuinely matters for two reasons. First, a show of ceremony sets the professional atmosphere necessary for trial. Secondly, because the jurors expect attorneys to follow certain formalities, the attorney disappoints the jury when he fails to participate in the ceremony.

An attorney's stating, "May it please the court . . . " immediately prior to delivering an opening statement or closing argument serves as one example of a tradition that serves no obvious purpose. The point is to respectfully ask the judge, "May I go ahead and do this now?" or "May I go ahead and handle this part of the trial a particular way?" Although these words are ceremonial in nature, the jury notices an attorney's failure to invoke them. And when this ritualistic language is used, attorneys show that they appreciate their proper role in the case by respecting the judge and, in doing so, respecting the process. Saying "may it please the court" does not necessarily contribute to the presentation of our cases. However, declining to utter these words causes jurors to wonder why the attorney chose not to participate in the formality. The jury often reaches the conclusion that the attorney is disrespectful and not taking the trial seriously. Distracting the jury undoubtedly detracts from our case.

Another example of a time-honored yet seemingly useless tradition is the chanting of "Oyez, oyez, oyez. Now rise for the judge" prior to attorneys presenting oral arguments before the Texas Supreme Court. Although merely ceremonial, the chant is not entirely without purpose. The chant helps to set a somber ambiance for the trial. Other formalities also encourage the jury to treat the trial as a solemn occasion and to approach the trial with a serious mindset. Our job is to not stand out. It is important to remember that we can stand out for being too casual or too rigid. Finding the right way to be comfortable in our skin while being respectful for the process is the trial lawyer's goal.

Jurors also expect attorneys to dress well for court. One juror suggested that an attorney less than well-dressed would prove distracting to the jury.

> *"They were both, in my mind, typically lawyer-dressed in three piece suits and ties. And so the appearance was not distracting. It was appropriate."*

When we fail to participate in formalities we do something inconsistent in the jurors' minds, thus detracting from our case. In *Rule 4: Set Expectations*, we will discuss how attorneys should set expectations for the jurors. In addition to the expectations that we set for them, jurors enter the courtroom with preconceived notions concerning how the trial ought to proceed. Jurors anticipate that lawyers will look and act a certain way. Jurors expect the attorneys to dress well, speak well, treat the judge respectfully, and to treat the witnesses respectfully.

Of course, form should never take precedence over substance. As attorneys, we should simply avoid acting too casually and not lose sight of the fact that our role in the courtroom truly makes a difference. Even if jurors have never set foot in a courthouse, they have expectations about how a trial court judge should be treated. Although the attorneys have probably had pre-trial interaction with the judge, the jurors don't necessarily know it; and they will not understand when lawyers carry over some animosity for the court due to an adverse pre-trial ruling. Our jurors told us repeatedly that there is one person in the courtroom who can do no wrong, and that person wears a black robe.

• *Respect the Judge*

Jurors believe that the best lawyers become judges. So the jurors believe the judge, by his or her very position, is smarter than the lawyers. More practically, to the jurors, the judge is the one who brings them donuts in the morning, and the bailiff is the one who helps them leave early when they need to pick up their kids. The attorney, on the other hand, is simply a hired gun. Once the trial begins, the rules of procedure prohibit attorneys from interacting with the jurors outside the courtroom or even off the record. The judge and his staff therefore have a much stronger rapport with the jury than the attorney does. The attorney should keep in mind how much more tenuous his relationship with the jurors is than the jurors' relationship with the judge or with the court staff when deciding how to treat the judge and court staff in front of the jury.

Not only do the jurors feel a stronger connection with the judge than with the attorney, but typically, they also assume the judge is always right. The thought that the judge's ruling may be erroneous or his assertions unfair rarely crosses the jurors' minds. Rather, the jurors tend to believe that the judge can do no wrong. Whenever a confrontation between the judge and an attorney arises, the jury usually or perhaps automatically takes the side of the judge. Therefore, when the judge reprimands an overly assertive attorney, the jury does not consider that the attorney may be in the right but rather assumes the attorney is out of line. One juror explained to us that an attorney's treating the judge with respect is simply common sense.

"I think the ideal lawyer would be someone who has enough sense, common sense, I mean—I don't think they teach it— but enough common sense to do just like the judge instructs, because the jury pays attention to the judge. And when the judge is disrespected by even a lawyer, it has something—it had more to do with me as a juror than the case in some points because after the judge told [the attorney] to settle down three times, I'm almost thinking, 'Why doesn't he just kick the case out?' Because the guy was definitely disrespectful to the judge, but the judge was really holding his ground."

Because the jury assumes that the judge is right, when there is a power struggle between the judge and the attorney or the judge's staff and the attorney, the judge (and by association, his staff) almost always wins. We rarely win battles against the judge; therefore, we best represent our clients by constantly venerating the judge in front of the jury.

Occasionally though, the jurors do perceive the judge as being unfair. In those rare situations, attorneys may benefit from standing up to the judge. However, because defying a judge in the jury's presence proves risky; when in doubt, we should assume that the jury has not turned on the judge and continue to treat the judge with the utmost respect.

Telling the judge that we are entitled to something or that the judge must do something is a dangerous proposition. Asserting that level of control is a bad idea, especially in the jury's presence. If we choose to be demanding, the judge had better agree with us. Otherwise, we risk losing the jury's respect. We are better off couching our arguments in the form of requests from the judge instead of demands.

Rather than commanding that "the judge must do this" or that "our client is entitled to that," we should frame our assertions in the form of requests. For example, if we believe that we are legally entitled to something, we should tell the judge, "In order to represent my client, I request X." Not only is a well-appeased judge more inclined to grant the attorney's request, but by making such requests, the attorney appears far more respectful to the jury than if he had stated, "I am entitled to X."

The lawyers, parties, witnesses, and jurors are all guests in the judge's courtroom. You show up when he tells you, you stand up when he tells you, you eat lunch when he tells you, and you talk on your cell phone if and when he tells you. Remember to act like a guest when you are in court and ask for permission at the appropriate times. Do not leave cups and papers everywhere—you wouldn't do that if you were staying in someone's home.

• *Treat the Court Staff as an Extension of the Judge*

The jury does not necessarily know what the bailiff, the court reporter, and the other members of the court staff actually do, but they can tell when a lawyer thinks he is better than they are. Even while attorneys are trying to ingratiate themselves with the jury, the jurors are watching to see how the attorneys are treating the court staff. Due in part to the fact that whenever the judge instructs a member of the court staff to do something, he immediately does it, the jury simply assumes that everyone in the courtroom works directly for the judge. In the minds of the jurors, the court staff shares the prestige of the robe. The attorney should therefore treat the court staff as an extension of the judge and with the greatest deference.

The Court Reporter: The attorney should never tell the court reporter to mark his exhibits. Both judges and juries absolutely hate it when lawyers treat court reporters like personal secretaries. The attorney should mark his own exhibits. Marking exhibits is part of the attorney's and his staff's job and does not fall within the court reporter's job description; therefore the attorney should not assume she is entitled to have the court reporter place stickers on her trial documents. It will be immediately apparent to the jurors whether the court reporter likes an attorney. If the court reporter does not like an attorney, the jurors might decide to follow his or her lead. A number of things can be done before trial to solidify your relationship with the court reporter. First, pay for transcripts on time. Second, ask her how she likes exhibits arranged. Most attorneys do not realize that official court reporters (yes, there is a such a thing as an unofficial one) have the statutory responsibility to memorialize everything that happens during a trial. She must get down everything that is said and possess every piece of evidence that is offered (even if it is not admitted) during the trial. This is a heavy and complicated responsibility and the players change for each trial. For this reason, ask the court reporter how she wants it done.

Court reporters typically do not do much talking during a trial, but they do a lot of listening, and they save their talking for the judge's chambers on breaks. If an attorney is not complying with a court reporter's expectations, the judge hears about it on the break or in the evening. The court reporter is the judge's eyes and ears in the courtroom; and when a judge is struggling with a legal or procedural issue, the court reporter will know it and be in a situation to influence the judge's decision. A happy court reporter means a happy judge which, in turn, usually means happy lawyers.

The Bailiff: It should go without saying that the person in the room with the badge and gun should be respected, but too often lawyers view the courtroom bailiff as an old, broken-down traffic cop. Even if the lawyers are correct, that old, broken-down traffic cop is the one who makes coffee for your jurors, makes sure their jury duty paychecks are properly processed, validates their parking for the discounted rate, makes lunch recommendations, and (sometimes not so subtly) tells them which lawyer knows what he's doing and which one doesn't. For elected judges, the jurors are potential voters who are going to leave the court and go back to their homes and jobs to tell other voters whether the judge knew what he was doing. The bailiff is the judge's ambassador to his jury (and voters who will help make sure the judge keeps his job at the next election). These facts should not be lost on the lawyer.

Bailiffs tell laudatory stories about their judges. Sometimes they are true. Jurors love the bailiff; and if they can tell the bailiff loves you, then it increases your credibility. Although the judge gets center stage, the bailiff is the one who really runs the show.

We must keep in mind that the bailiff is not an attorney's gopher. Many attorneys make the mistake of ordering the bailiff around. For example, an attorney might tell the bailiff to go fetch him the easel. Not only does an attorney's giving the bailiff orders greatly irritate both the bailiff and the judge, but it also immensely bothers the jury. The bailiff is often responsible for the document camera, the projector, and the lighting in the courtroom. Checking with the bailiff before trial starts and at each break to tell him your needs will make your trial smoother. Many lawyers are surprised to learn bailiffs have substantial administrative duties related to making the court run smoothly. The bailiff retrieves the hearing and trial dockets, calls jurors from the central jury room, completes reports for county auditors, and does anything else the judge requests. It does not make the bailiff happy when you interrupt his administrative work during trial to help you fix a self-created emergency with the document camera and projector. It is important to respect his job responsibilities too.

Because the jury views the bailiff and the court reporter as extensions of the judge, a good rule of thumb is to not command the court reporter or the bailiff to do anything we would not tell the judge to do. Would you direct the judge to mark your exhibits? Would you instruct him to retrieve a piece of equipment for you? I think not. Therefore we should not instruct members of the court staff to do so. We should treat the court staff with courtesy and respect. For example, instead of telling the court reporter to mark our exhibits, we should address the judge and say something along the lines of "Your Honor, I don't have my stickers—may I ask the court reporter for some?" Also, rather than demanding that the bailiff bring us the easel, try self help and ask the judge, "Your

Honor, may I grab the easel?" When the attorney phrases his need in the form of a respectful request, as opposed to a demanding order, the court staff is more inclined to help.

Much of the time, court staff members simply want to do things their own way and are far more receptive to a courteous attorney than to a self-entitled one. We need to do our jobs, and we need to allow the court staff to do theirs. By treating the court staff as an extension of the judge, we contribute to the jury's perception that we as attorneys respect the process.

• *Treat Witnesses with Respect*

The jury expects lawyers to treat every person in the courtroom with dignity. This is especially true when it comes to witnesses—even adverse witnesses. Jurors tend to identify with witnesses as opposed to attorneys. This is in part due to humanity's pervasive fear of public speaking or being put on the spot to answer questions. Jurors readily empathize with the individual (a novice to the process) on the stand whom the attorney (an experienced veteran) is grilling. Jurors more readily visualize themselves in the witness chair than behind the podium. When the attorney rakes the witness over the coals, the jury's initial reaction is not to find the attorney and his questioning clever but to sympathize with the poor, abused witness. Therefore, when the attorney mistreats the witness, the jury becomes upset and even irate. One juror expressed dislike for an attorney's becoming combative with a witness.

"You particularly don't want the attorneys to get combative with the witnesses. That really doesn't fly well."

We need to examine every witness in a professional fashion, even if we believe the witness is a big, fat liar. Because jurors usually relate far more to witnesses than to attorneys, we do ourselves no favors by demeaning witnesses.

• *Treat Opposing Counsel with Respect*

The attorney should even treat opposing counsel with respect. Neither the judge nor the jury likes an attorney who acts discourteously toward opposing counsel or opposing counsel's client. One juror expressed his appreciation for a judge's reacting harshly to an attorney who made a side comment to the attorney for the other side during trial.

"One thing that I think all of us talked about in the jury room is when the defense lawyer made an aside comment to the prosecuting attorney, and the judge called him down on it. And that was kind of—it was surprising. First of all that [the defense lawyer] made the comment. And it was, secondly, surprising the harshness with which it was dealt with. It was a good thing that it was dealt with severely but it surprised me that it was."

There is literally no upside to treating people poorly. When we are rude to others, it reflects badly on us in the eyes of the jury. One juror told us that when the attorney makes arrogant remarks to a witness or snide comments to opposing counsel, the attorney comes across as cocky and unprofessional. We should also be careful not to be too familiar with our adversary because jurors don't know what to make of this. If they see us joking around with opposing counsel, they might question the sincerity of our presentation at trial.

"I found [the attorney] at times to seem kind of a little bit cocky. A little bit—some of the remarks he made just seemed kind of a little arrogant. I can't remember exactly what they were, but I remember thinking at the time they seemed a little inappropriate. There was one to the witness. And there was one situation—I can't remember exactly what it was, but it was something he said to the other attorney. And it just kind of caught me off guard. It didn't seem very professional."

• *Treat Your Staff with Respect*

We must treat our staff as part of our team not as our minions. Jurors distinctly notice when we are unkind or condescending to our clerks and associates. When the attorney acts kindly to the jury but disrespectfully to his staff, the attorney appears duplicitous. By treating our staff with respect, we maintain our integrity. One juror explained to us how much it bothered and distracted him when a senior associate required a member of his team to sit, not at counsel table, but in the back of the courtroom.

> *"[The plaintiff's lawyer] had what I believe to be was his clerk who he didn't have near him. He had him sit back in the gallery seats, and so there would be a lot of looking around—fluttering for papers or asking for things—which just seemed sort of awkward. It was kind of disrespectful. It's kind of like if he's part of your team, shouldn't he have been there with you? And, you know, it seemed kind of odd how they interacted."*

Let this be a reminder of how much attention juries pay to details—including how you treat your own team. Next time you find yourself barking "Get me Exhibit 12!" you might stop yourself and ask "Ms. Cassidy, will you please put up Exhibit 12?"

In addition to treating junior associates and employees with respect, senior lawyers should avoid distracting the jury by reprimanding or advising younger associates who are in the process of examining a witness or making an objection. I cannot tell you how many times I saw this when I was on the bench. A senior lawyer shoves notes in front of a younger lawyer in the middle of an examination. This is probably not helpful to the attorney. It distracts him and breaks the flow of his examination. If seasoned attorneys choose to work with younger ones, they need to treat them as part of their team and show them trust and respect. The jury understands that the A-Team cannot do all of the work—not all witnesses are A-Team witnesses. The jury also understands that the younger attorneys are less experienced than older attorneys. The older lawyer needs to avoid hassling the younger associates and let them do their jobs.

Rule 2:
Be Prepared

Benjamin Franklin said, "By failing to prepare, you are preparing to fail." While Franklin wasn't a lawyer, his advice is applicable to trial law. Over the years I have learned there is simply no substitute for hard work in trial law. Whether it is giving a flawless opening or pinning an adverse witness on cross examination, you have to know your record, know the facts, know every conceivable place the witness may run, and know how you will corral him.

• *There Is No Substitute for Preparation*

We all want to succeed. We all want to win for our clients. Yet very few people possess the willpower to put forth the time and effort to turn their desires into reality. As legendary Alabama football coach Bear Bryant aptly phrased it: "It's not the will to win that matters . . . everyone has that; it's the will to prepare to win that matters." For the trial attorney, there is simply no substitute for hard work and preparation. Preparation truly separates the excellent attorney from the mediocre one.

I remember well my first trial in federal court. I had picked up the case and the client as a result of one of the senior partners leaving the firm. I was defending my client against allegations of multi-million dollar fraud and breach of contract in a case involving the manufacture of 75 different computer circuit boards. The case was factually a mess because it arose under the UCC and started with a master contract that was supplemented or amended with the boilerplate terms on the back of the purchase orders and acceptances exchanged by the parties with each succeeding order.

I had been practicing for only four years, and I was staring down the thirty-day barrel of a two-week trial in federal court. I remember wondering how I was going to make sense of, much less pull a reasoned and principled theme out of, the thousands of pages of exhibits and twenty-five depositions in the case. The answer I found was many long nights of reviewing documents and digesting depositions to synthesize a reasoned and principled basis upon which the jury could side with my client. It was hard and long but there really is no other way to do it. No matter how intelligent or articulate you are, there is no other way to pull all of the factual threads into a comprehensive tapestry of a trial presentation except hard work. At the end of the day, the preparation paid off. The jury returned a take-nothing verdict after three days of deliberation.

I know my experience is not unique. Mike McKool, an incredibly successful intellectual property trial attorney in Dallas, serves as a further example that there is no substitute for hard work and preparation. A local magazine did a profile of Mike, which I kept because in the interview he explained that prior to a trial he would cloister himself in a hotel room for days or even weeks, where he did nothing except eat a little, sleep a little, and pour over the evidence until he knew his case inside and out. McKool is very intelligent and good on his feet, but he attributes his success in the courtroom to something else: methodical preparation. Preparation pays off with juries most of all. To jurors, an attorney is only as persuasive as he is prepared. One of the jurors we interviewed, who speaks publicly for a living and therefore has specialized insight on this very issue, explained that there is a direct correlation between preparation and the speaker's ability to convince or persuade.

"An attorney is only going to be as persuasive as the facts and his preparation. And I speak in front of groups of people frequently in my job, and the most successful presentations are the ones that you know inside and out, so you can't be too prepared."

There are three reasons a prepared attorney is an impressive attorney and worthy of the jury's attention. The first and most obvious is that preparation ensures that you know everything about the record so that no fact can or will surprise you, and no legal issue will arise for which you are unprepared. The second is the effect that it has on you, the trial lawyer. You are confident in yourself because you know that you are completely and thoroughly familiar with the record. If a witness misstates a fact, you know which exhibit to use in correcting that point. If your adversary raises an objection to one of your documents, you are prepared with a response and basis to admit the exhibit. The jury will sense this confidence and appreciate it as conviction and a sincere belief that your client is in the right. The third and ultimate benefit of preparation is that it will earn you the respect and attention of the jury. When the jury sees how well you know the record and the law, the jury becomes confident that they can rely on what you say. You have proven to be a knowledgeable and credible guide for the case. The next time you rise to speak, the jury will listen—and listen attentively—because they are confident that you know what you are talking about. Once you have won the jury's confidence, they will perceive everything you do on your client's behalf in a more favorable light.

Anyone who has tried a case knows that once the trial gets started, things will become wild and wooly; everything does not go perfectly every time. There will be hiccups. The prepared attorney builds equity in the bank with the jury for those moments when things do not go perfectly. In the event that something fails to go according to plan, the jury will give the prepared attorney some leeway. For example, when an attorney is punctual ten days in a row but on the eleventh day runs five minutes late, the jury will be more inclined to cut him some slack. On the other hand, jurors have no sympathy for the frequently tardy attorney. The frequently tardy attorney has lost the confidence of the jury and often their willingness to bear with and pay attention through his delays and missteps. Likewise, when an attorney has been cordial and professional to the judge, the bailiff, the court reporter, and opposing counsel, the jury is more forgiving when something unforeseen occurs. On the other hand, if the attorney has been arrogant and condescending to others in the courtroom, the jurors will be far less likely to give the attorney the benefit of the doubt and, at times, they may even enjoy seeing an attorney flounder.

One variation on this theme we have seen in the courtroom is what to do if your adversary has problems with equipment. Should you let him flounder or should you step in and help? Some will say just let him flounder. It is his problem and he should have to deal with it. We actually suggest a different approach. Look at it as another opportunity to draw a contrast between your preparation and competence. Think about it. If you step in and solve the problems, you do get him out of the pinch; but at the same time, you make yourself look like a stand-up guy who knows what he is doing. Aiding opposing counsel expedites the trial; and more importantly, makes attorneys seem like understanding human beings. We gain nothing from being unhelpful; and what goes around, comes around. If I've been obliging and agreeable when my opponent has difficulties, the judge is more likely to cut me some slack in the event of my own technical failure. When an attorney has been unwilling to help, the judge will probably apply the mantra "live by the sword, die by the sword" and strictly enforce the rules against the difficult and unaccommodating attorney. Plus, don't your efforts to assist your adversary through his technical difficulties also send the unspoken message that you are not afraid of anything he is going to say or do? You are glad to help him out because no matter what he does your client is right and will prevail. In the end, assisting your adversary demonstrates the supreme confidence you have in your case.

In the remainder of this chapter, we'll discuss several specific things—small but noticeable things—you can do to demonstrate that you are entirely prepared to present your case.

• *Be on Time*

I have to confess, this is one of my pet peeves. I do not believe in being on time; I believe in being early. The reason is simple—respect. How do you feel when you are kept waiting in a doctor's office or waiting and in the dark about whether your plane is going to leave on time or whether you will be stuck in Newark overnight? It makes you unhappy. It makes you unhappy because you feel ignored. The person you are waiting for does not appreciate or value your time. Jurors are no different. They have lives, spouses, families, and jobs that they are spending time away from to serve as the decision-makers in your trial. When you are late, you are telling them they are less important than you are.

We should approach court attendance with the same respect with which we treat wedding attendance. When two people plan to exchange vows, the wedding party, the clergy, and the invitees all make sure to arrive early or precisely on time. No one would dare walk into a chapel right before the bride started down the aisle. I am sure there are things more disrespectful, but this has got to be pretty high on the list. Just as a person would avoid walking into a wedding after it has started, the attorney should never arrive late to court.

The tardy attorney insults the jury by sending a message that his time is more important than that of the twelve of them combined. Everyone in the courtroom (except the jurors) has a direct incentive to be there. The clients are there for the trial of their case, in which they have direct financial interest. The bailiff, the court reporter, and even the judge are paid to attend trial. The jury assumes the attorneys are being very well compensated—whether that is true or not. The jurors have less at stake than anyone else. For the grand sum of $40.00 a day, they are required to sit through every minute of the trial. As attorneys, the least we can do is ensure that we arrive on time.

"Yes," you tell me, "but the judge is late all the time." That is different and it does not matter. Though a judge's lack of timeliness may annoy the jury, the jury quickly will forgive the man or woman in the black robe. He has the power to order them pizza for lunch and let them go early on Friday. He can make up for any past transgressions because it is his courtroom. Besides, as a general principle in the jurors' minds, the judge can do no wrong. Don't think for a second that this applies to attorneys. The jury simply will not tolerate an attorney's habitual tardiness.

And if the jury does not get you for being late, the judge will. One of the state judges in Dallas has a specific policy aimed at trial lawyers who show up late for trial. The first time you run late, the court and jury wait for you but when you arrive, you get a stern warning about your tardiness. The second time you run late, the judge and jury will wait for you, but this time you are told that there will be no more waiting, and court will proceed without you. If you are late a third time, the show goes on without you.

• *Have Your Witnesses Ready*

This is a simple one, but you would be surprised how many times attorneys run afoul of it. You always need to have your next witness— and perhaps your next two witnesses—ready to go.

Jury duty is truly a sacrifice for the jurors; it forces them away from caring for their sick mothers, attending after-school activities with their children, and a litany of other activities that they would rather be doing. Considering that jurors have more pressing matters in life to attend to than our trials, jurors find it unforgiveable when an attorney is not well organized enough to present a cohesive case.

Think of yourself and the presentation of your case as if you were the director of all activities—because, in fact, you are. In theater, the director is responsible for putting on a flawless production. To do so, he must synchronize actors, scene changes, props, and costumes. The director must constantly be on the ball; he must know what comes next in the play and perfectly coordinate it. Like theater directors, attorneys are responsible for presenting a seamless case. Our job entails ensuring that the trial runs smoothly, which includes coordinating trial exhibits and witnesses. We need to have all of our documents in order and ensure that the witnesses are lined up and ready to perform on their stage—the witness stand.

When we finish examining a witness at four in the afternoon, we either need to have another witness lined up and ready to go or we need to be prepared to rest our case. At four p.m., the jury is present and scheduled to receive another hour or so of evidence. The court is expecting you to make good use of all the time the day has to offer. Neither the judge nor the jury will appreciate the attorney's prolonging the trial simply because he does not have another witness ready to call, and both will hold the attorney accountable in some way. The mantra of theater production is "the show must go on." The same is true in the courtroom. Regardless of whether the next witness is ready, the trial must continue.

The attorney without a witness to present is like the director without an actor to go on stage. The entire play or trial comes to a screeching, fumbling, "excuse me" halt. It will continue, but it will not be a smooth or pleasant experience. A federal judge we know, when faced with an attorney without a witness ready to go, ends the attorney's case right there, whether the attorney was ready to close or not. Our advice is make sure that you have your next witness (and maybe next two witnesses) out in the hall, waiting to go. We also like to keep the two witnesses after that on a two-hour call, meaning they have promised us that if we call them, they will be at the courthouse in less than two hours.

• *Prepare in Advance to Expedite the Trial*

We need to plan each trial with as much precision as the Royal Wedding planners coordinated the union of Prince William and Kate Middleton. The Royal Wedding planners considered every detail when organizing the grand event. The planners predetermined how long it would take the Queen to walk down the aisle, how many people would attend, and at what time the balcony kiss would occur. Likewise, attorneys need to accurately determine in advance how long it will take to examine each witness, how many exhibits we will enter into evidence, and in what order we will present our trial to the jury. Unfortunately, attorneys typically do not plan as fastidiously as we should.

The more time we take to present our case, the more likely our jurors will feel that we wasted their time. We compound the jurors' "you-are-wasting-my-time" feeling even further if we (as attorneys often do) repeat ourselves.

We never want to leave a juror feeling like this. The logic behind this is pretty straightforward. When someone repeats something to you not once, not twice, but three times, you automatically start thinking, "I don't like this guy. With all this repeating, he must think I am an idiot." Jurors are just like you and me in this respect. As a lawyer, I do not guarantee much; but I will guarantee you this: If your actions cause the twelve people in the jury box to have this thought about you, then things won't go too well for you and your client in deliberations.

When we blatantly disrespect the jurors' time or take actions that signal that we think jurors are slow or stupid, the jurors are likely to visit their anger on our cases. To avoid wasting the jury's time, we need to ensure that the case moves as rapidly as possible. To expedite the trial, we should logistically prepare in every way possible. Numerous jurors have expressed that they want attorneys to do as much prep work as we can prior to the commencement of trial. One juror, who works in the theater industry, told us that by getting the administrative details out of the way beforehand, the attorney tries the most efficient case possible.

"I work in theater and so I'm visual and everything is rehearsed. The more you can get out of the way in terms of prep and making sure everything works the way it's intended to work beforehand, the better, so you're giving your cleanest, most efficient, and direct case possible and not wasting anybody's time."

And if this is how the jurors perceive your actions in the courtroom, how much of your message do you think they are getting?

One of the biggest time drains in trial is admitting exhibits. If you use the techniques that you were taught in a trial advocacy class—hand the exhibit to the court reporter, ask her to mark it, give it to your opponent, give it to the witness, ask your foundation questions, then offer the exhibit—you will bore the jury to death. One technique you can use to bypass this monotonous and archaic litany is by pre-marking and pre-admitting exhibits. Before the trial, spend time with opposing counsel and agree on the exhibits and get them pre-admitted. When it comes time for trial, everyone has a copy of everything that was pre-admitted; and then outside the presence of the jury, you can move to admit all of those exhibits before the trial starts. By pre-marking and pre-admitting evidence, we avoid unnecessarily subjecting the jury to dull administrative tasks.

We also suggest using a numbering system in the deposition phase of the case that will make your trial preparation efforts more efficient. How many times have you gotten to the end of a case and realized that during the course of depositions you marked thirteen different Exhibit 1s—essentially a new "Exhibit 1" for each deposition that you took. This is confusing and it makes it impossible to follow if you ever want to use deposition testimony with an exhibit at trial, because none of the numbers match up. And who wants to spend his time in front of the jury explaining that what the witness referred to as "Exhibit 1" is really trial Exhibit 43? You can avoid all this hassle in your next case by agreeing with your adversary that all deposition exhibits will be numbered consecutively. At your first deposition, mark the first exhibit number "1," then number every exhibit thereafter sequentially, whether it is in that deposition or the ones that follow. When it comes time for trial you simply select the exhibits that you want for trial, and they are all pre-numbered. If you have any additional exhibits to mark—and both sides usually do—then just allocate a different group of exhibit numbers to each party. For example, if 250 exhibits were marked in the depositions, then the plaintiff can add exhibits 251 to 350 and the defendant can have exhibits 351 to 450. Alternatively, the plaintiff could mark his exhibits as plaintiff's exhibits while the defendant labels his as defendant's exhibits. Planning simple details, such as how to mark exhibits, facilitates a smooth running trial.

Bringing a sufficient number of exhibit copies to trial can also expedite the process. We suggest making copies for you, the judge, opposing counsel, the court reporter, and the witnesses. For each witness, you should consider preparing a binder that contains only the narrow set of exhibits you intend to use with that witness. For example, if there are 300 exhibits in the case, but you will only use 12 with a given witness, providing him with a single binder of all his exhibits will save a lot of flipping through pages while the witness looks for the right exhibit. This type of logistics planning means that the trial will run smoother and more efficiently. It is also more respectful of jurors' time. If, in contrast to our detailed preparation, opposing counsel fails to do simple things such as pre-admitting exhibits or making small notebooks of particular exhibits, we look even better by comparison.

• *Admit Exhibits Efficiently*

Ideally, opposing counsel will agree to the authenticity and admissibility of all our exhibits. Should opposing counsel decline, we need a plan for getting each document into evidence. Formulating a strategy for getting documents admitted avoids fumbling around and potentially failing to get the documents into evidence.

If we have not already gotten a document into evidence, we should lead with issues of authenticity and admissibility. Under Texas Rule of Evidence 104, the rules of evidence do not bind the judge when he determines whether evidence is admissible. Although the judge can certainly overrule us, asking the witness whether he recognizes the document we want to get admitted sufficiently authenticates the document. If the judge is dissatisfied with our simply asking the witness, "Do you recognize this document?" we should lay the full predicate but do so as succinctly as possible.

The process of admitting documents seems fussy and antiquated to jurors. Take the business records predicate for example—the predicate consists of four or five questions, depending on how it is broken up. Unless the attorney prepares his witness, the witness has no idea what the attorney is getting at with his odd, out-of-place questions. The business records predicate also puzzles the jury. The jury wonders what the seemingly random questions have to do with the case at hand or with the price of tea in China for that matter. When we ask the witness strange and apparently irrelevant questions, the jury zones out and stops listening to our examination.

If forced to lay the business records predicate, we should ask all of the questions at once instead of breaking the inquiry into multiple questions. We should ask "was the record made at or near the time of the events or conditions recorded, kept in the course of business, by someone whose business it was to keep the records?" By forcing the predicate into one question, we minimize the jury's tendency to tune us out.

Ask opposing counsel to agree to business records. If opposing counsel refuses, then we can readily get the records into evidence by simply asking the four or five required questions, making opposing counsel appear petty to the jury and ridiculous to the judge. On the flipside, do not object unnecessarily to the other side's evidence.

Unless there is a genuinely good reason to object to the other side's evidence—for example, it proves unreliable due to hearsay or a lack of authenticity—then let his or her evidence in. Only pick fights you can win. If opposing counsel's evidence is clearly and undoubtedly admissible, you shouldn't object. By readily agreeing to our adversary's evidence, we appear confident in our case and send a message to the jury that nothing that our opponent is doing is affecting our case or our belief that we should prevail.

• *Let Co-Counsel and the Client in on the Story*

When multiple attorneys work together on a case, they need to present a united front. By appearing to work together, the attorneys come across to the jury as well organized for trial. On the other hand, when attorneys on the same side of the case fuss with one another, the jurors view them as unprepared. One juror suggested that feuding attorneys on the same side of the case are distracting.

> *"There were two—it was him and it seemed like a junior partner or something like that, and so they both did different things in the case and seemed to trade off and seemed to be on the same page with each other, so there wasn't those type of distractions."*

Remember our director analogy? There are many different actors, but it is our job to make sure all actors play their parts and work well together. If we do not, then our clients will suffer.

The same principle applies to your relationship with your client. We need to appear to be on the same page as our clients. Disorganization and notes constantly being passed between counsel and client suggest something is wrong in paradise. Juries see everything, and they are sure to see any snags in your relationship with your client if they take place in the courtroom. According to one juror, when a client argues with his own attorney, that side of the case seems unready for trial.

> *"The main plaintiff—now that it's coming back to me—did not seem like they had rehearsed. It didn't go well. I mean, just the plaintiff seemed sometimes to be adversarial with his own lawyer. That was weird. He didn't seem like they had planned well with him."*

Here is a juror wondering how there can be a disagreement between an attorney and his client. We all know that trials are heated battles, and lots of things go on in trial—sometimes unexpected things—but you cannot let these displays occur in the courtroom in the presence of the jury.

We also need to keep our clients well informed of the proceedings so that the clients do not appear surprised. Jurors carefully watch the clients and thoroughly contemplate their facial expressions. When the client seems shocked by questions asked or surprised by documents admitted, the client and his attorney seem unprepared for the case and therefore less credible.

• *Avoid Technical Problems*

If you intend to use technical equipment as part of your case, you need to ensure that it works properly prior to bringing the jury into the courtroom. The jury has absolutely no desire to watch the attorney fumbling to turn on the overhead projector or trying to cue a video to the appropriate place in a deposition. One juror expressed frustration at having to watch the attorneys ready the technical equipment.

> *"I felt that the information could have been presented a little more efficiently and expediently. There are items that have been rehearsed and/or set up before they were being presented —meaning the equipment should have been ready to go. It should have been cued—hit a button—instead of fumbling around to try to get the computer to where it needed to be."*

When the equipment fails, jurors never blame the judge or the courthouse staff. The jury neither knows nor cares that the equipment belongs to the court or that the attorney tried his best to get the equipment to function. The jury holds the attorney responsible for technical glitches. With this in mind, we bring our own equipment to court. If we opt to roll the dice and use government equipment, we need to have a contingency plan. For example, if we plan to use a PowerPoint presentation, we should bring hard copies of all our slides just in case something goes wrong.

Even when we do everything possible to prevent technical problems, they inevitably occur. We cannot sit idly by or ask for a break whenever a technical issue arises. Rather, we must immediately acknowledge the situation to the judge and to the jury. Ask the judge for five minutes to fix the glitch. If the problem cannot be remedied quickly or if the judge declines permission, we must be prepared to continue with the case.

Rule 3:
Be Credible

From the moment the venire walks into the courtroom for voir dire, your jury is among them, already comparing the credibility of the lawyers. A crude but powerful analogy describes the importance of credibility: "Credibility is like virginity; once you lose it, it is impossible to get back." Most jurors are not familiar with the legal process associated with a jury trial so they are looking for a leader to be their guide. They want a guide to tell them how long the journey will take, who they will meet along the way, and what they can expect. Your goal as the trial lawyer is to become that guide. The guide who earns the jury's trust becomes a credible advocate with substantial influence over how the jury views the evidence and, eventually, how the jury answers the questions in the verdict form.

This begs the question: What makes a trial lawyer credible to jurors? Two things we have already discussed—respect for the process and preparation—are cornerstones of credibility. Keep in mind, jurors, like all of us, have friends, advisors, and bosses, plus a lifetime of experiences with these and other people. Our jurors told us that the same things that make a person credible outside the courtroom also make a trial lawyer credible in the courtroom.

• *Your First Impression*

They say "you never get a second chance to make a good first impression," and this is especially true in court. Credibility is about trust. When a person is credible, we believe what she has to say. Over time, we begin to trust her judgment; that is, we believe the facts she tells us. We also more easily accept the conclusions she has reached after analyzing those facts. Social psychologists have identified trust-building behaviors that create trust and establish credibility that are applicable both inside and outside the courtroom.

Taking a business example, trust is developed when someone shows up early, is prepared to get to work, achieves the objective, and comes in under budget. Why is that? Because the person has met or exceeded expectations. Throughout this book we talk about setting and meeting expectations. Building credibility with jurors is about meeting and, whenever possible, exceeding their expectations.

Jurors expect us to show up on time and be prepared for trial. If we continually fumble and repeatedly make mistakes, the jury grows reluctant to give us their attention. Why? Because our fumbling and missteps are wasting their time. If you do it too often, you not only lose your jury at that moment, you condition them to tune you out next time because you are not worth their time. In short, you get written off. The jurors only give the attorney so many opportunities before withdrawing their attention. By stumbling over words and searching for exhibits, a lawyer with a good case will distract jurors and detract from his case.

"Whereas the other attorney talked to us, and I felt like he probably had a good case, but he fumbled. And I think that took away, and I don't think that he wasn't prepared. Sometimes he would stumble over his words or his exhibits would be—what he was presenting is not what he had told us he was going to present. So his presentation—it was almost like he hadn't practiced enough or he hadn't gone over exactly what he was going to say."

People outside the courtroom also give one another only a limited number of chances to do something properly before dismissing them permanently. Take friends A and B for example. If A asked B to do his laundry and B agreed, A would expect that B would: (1) separate the clothes properly, (2) wash them with detergent, (3) dry them, and (4) fold them neatly. If instead, B: (1) mixes the red laundry with the white, (2) decides against adding soap, and (3) returns the clothes in a wet, wrinkled heap, A would never again ask B to help him with the laundry. At that point, even if B got down on his knees and begged for the opportunity to do A's laundry, A would decline—B has already proven himself incapable of washing clothes.

The Boy Who Cried Wolf is the classic example of how a person only gets so many chances before others write him off. According to the fable, a shepherd boy, whose occupation was to alert the villagers of impending wolves, cried "Wolf!" when no wolf approached. The villagers came running, noticed the absence of a wolf and found themselves somewhat less than amused. Later, despite the lack of a wolf again, the boy cried "Wolf!" another time. Much to their chagrin, the villagers came running a second time. After the boy's alerts proved blatantly wrong yet again, the townspeople wrote him off and refused to listen to any additional warnings. Although the boy eventually did have something legitimate and well worth listening to say—a wolf finally did come to collect his prey—it was too late, as the villagers had already decided that the boy did not deserve their attention.

Just as B deterred A from asking B to help with his laundry by doing a poor job and just as the boy who cried wolf discouraged the townspeople from coming to the sheep's aid with false alarms, the attorney deters the jury from listening to him by repeatedly screwing up. The jury expects a sensible, well-rehearsed presentation of the evidence and becomes impatient with an attorney who constantly bumbles. We avoid fumbling by simply preparing well for our cases and remaining calm, collected, and professional during trial. Jurors expect lawyers to make eye contact, stand up straight with good posture, project their voice in a confident manner so the jury can hear them, and dress in a professional manner. Jurors also expect us to know the facts of our case.

> *"You know, this guy has been working on this for six or seven years, and he had stacks and stacks of stuff. How he could have missed—and I don't remember exactly what this one thing was, but it was like how did he miss that? And it had to do with her medical records or something like that... And he could have still won—that wouldn't have made me decide any different—but, you know, in my mind I'm thinking he's not really got it all together."*

These remarks really summarize a lot of the things we have been discussing. The juror expects the lawyer, as a professional who has worked on the case for six to seven years, to know about all the documents. In reality, who knows how long this lawyer had been involved in the case or what the status of discovery was. Regardless, the point remains: to be a credible advocate you have to know the case as if you had lived it for seven years.

• *Be Professional at All Times*

It is not just the first impression that is important because the jury is always watching. You are on display from the moment the trial process begins. Jurors park in the same garage as the attorneys, parties, and witnesses. If you drive like a jerk, the jurors will notice. If your client drives a bright yellow Lamborghini, the jurors will notice. If you use foul language when you are talking with one of your partners while walking through the parking garage one afternoon, the jurors will hear you. It only takes one. If one juror hears or sees you doing something, soon the entire jury will know. Remember, they cannot talk about the subject of the trial, but the attorney's behavior is fair game and in fact, can become a quite popular topic of discussion among the jurors.

Once the trial starts, the attorney is continually on display for the jury. Nosy and inquisitive, the jurors carefully observe the attorney in an endeavor to most accurately ascertain the attorney's character. The jurors watch every time we stand up, each time we walk through the halls, and sometimes even as we park our cars. Because the jurors constantly and meticulously scrutinize the attorney, she must be professional at all times and not just while in the courtroom addressing the jurors.

How we act while not addressing the jury is perhaps more crucial than how we carry ourselves while communicating to the jury. Many jurors believe the mantra "integrity is who you are when no one is watching" applies to trial litigation. The jurors undoubtedly recognize that the attorney is acutely aware that the jurors carefully scrutinize his behavior and demeanor while he addresses them in the courtroom and is therefore on his best behavior in front of the jury. The jury also unquestionably understands that a person's true colors tend to show when the person is unaware that he is under the magnifying glass. Therefore, we need to assume that we are being observed at all times and exude professionalism always—this is especially the case when we walk the halls, park our cars, and ride the elevator.

• *Demonstrate Knowledge of Court Rules and Courtroom Practices*

Jurors expect attorneys to act like they belong in the courtroom. When an attorney offers evidence, the typical juror has no real understanding of what the attorney is doing. For the most part, the jury finds predicates insignificant, and attorney's stating, "I offer Exhibit X into evidence" hardly worthy of a yawn. When the offering process goes smoothly, the jury is mostly unaware of an attorney's asking predicate questions or his offering exhibits. However, although the jurors do not listen intently to an attorney's offering evidence, the jury most certainly notices when the attorney stammers and bobbles. Fumbling and stuttering while trying to admit evidence negatively reflects on him and diminishes his credibility.

The process of admitting evidence is one of the basics of the legal process which the jurors expect trial attorneys to know cold. When the attorney appears unfamiliar with fundamental trial procedure, the jury finds him incompetent. By mastering the art of offering evidence, we appear as though we frequent the courtroom and know what we are doing. The jury finds the competent attorney credible; therefore, we increase our credibility with the jury by admitting evidence cleanly.

Jurors also pay attention to whether the lawyer is comfortable interacting with the judge and opposing counsel. Jurors do not expect a "you can't handle the truth" moment during witness examination, but they do understand that the process is adversarial. Jurors understand that on certain points the lawyers will not agree; and in appropriate circumstances, the judge may not like or agree with something a lawyer is doing. To that end, a credible lawyer is able to hold his ground with the judge and opposing counsel while remaining professional.

The attorney should appear at home in the courtroom. When she seems comfortable with the legal process, the jury finds her competent. By taking control of the courtroom, the attorney inspires confidence and fosters respect. The attorney should be as self-sufficient as possible to appear in charge of the trial.

On the other hand, the attorney wants to avoid stepping on the judge's toes. In the minds of the jurors, the judge is king of the courtroom and the attorney a mere minion. As king of the courtroom, the judge can do no wrong. When the judge grows frustrated and yells at the attorney for failing to follow his particular courtroom methods, the jurors find the attorney careless and disrespectful.

The attorney strikes a good balance between taking control of the courtroom and not incurring the judge's wrath for failing to oblige the judge's idiosyncrasies by becoming familiar with the judge, his preferences, and his courtroom procedures. Several jurors have informed us that the trial attorney who understands what the judge will and will not allow comes across as better prepared than the attorney who does not. One juror told us:

> *"I think if the attorney is better prepared, understands—and it's not saying not understanding the law but really kind of understanding what the judge is probably going to allow and not allow which it seems like the larger firm does have. Whereas the other attorney is more of a hem-haw type of situation and doesn't seem to be as controlled in that part."*

First of all, we must determine whether the judge permits us to approach the witness without asking. Second, we need to be considerate of the court reporter. As stated earler, do not ask the court reporter to mark an exhibit and then continue examining witnesses or making motions. The court reporter has taken an oath to transcribe everything said during trial and cannot do so when we ask her to do two things at once. If unable to pre-admit an exhibit, we should respectfully tell the judge, "Your Honor, I need the court reporter to mark an exhibit, so let me know when we get to a stopping point so she can quit typing and mark the exhibit."

• *Know What You're Going to Say Before You Say It*

As attorneys, we need to plan every detail of the case prior to the commencement of trial. Jurors expect attorneys to appear well-rehearsed and as though they have planned what to say in advance. When the attorney exudes readiness, he comes across to the jurors as slick in a positive way. On the other hand, the attorney who appears to ask questions to kill time does not come across well to the jurors. As one juror aptly phrased it:

> *"The defendant's attorney—he was just slick. I mean, he had a way of speaking that was just—it's hard to explain, but he knew what he was going to say before he ever said it. And he was—he didn't drone on about things. He just got right to the point, asked his questions, and all of them seemed to matter. They were not just asking questions to kill time or whatever. It seemed like the other guy did that from time to time so he could thumb through some of his notes. [The defendant's attorney] was just way more concise in the way he spoke and the questions that he asked. He just seemed like he knew what he was doing."*

Again, preparation and confidence in your case leaves jurors with a favorable and positive impression.

• *Earn and Keep the Jurors' Attention*

Jurors do not grant their undivided attention automatically—lawyers must earn it. And once we gain the jurors' attention, we must work consistently to retain it. Part of keeping the jurors' attention is speaking clearly, concisely, and with readily understandable language. The exceedingly verbose attorney who utilizes a dictionary of large, intelligent-sounding words quickly loses the jury's focus. Although we may seem clever when we show off our vocabulary, we also come across as arrogant individuals to whom the jury cannot relate. To the average juror, lofty language either proves entirely incomprehensible or incredibly difficult to dissect. We should keep in mind that the jurors have absolutely no vested interest in our cases and have no compelling reason to put forth a great deal of effort simply to understand what the attorney says.

To develop rapport with the jury, the attorney needs to ensure that the jury can relate to him. Jurors have a difficult time relating to an attorney whose language they cannot follow. Jurors have expressed that they appreciate when the attorney plainly explains the case without being condescending. One juror told us that by talking in laymen's terms, the attorney communicates effectively.

> *"Just talk to us in laymen's terms, because there's some people who don't have education. I have education, but some people don't have education, and you don't want to confuse the jury. You want them to understand that—you want them to know what's going on without confusing them, because you'll lose them."*

The attorney's goal is to explain his case to the jury in a way that they can clearly understand. One juror praised an attorney for his crisp questions and effective method of communication.

> *"Next, the defense attorney, in my mind, he was the most effective. And the reason being is, for one thing, he was a little bit more understated. For another thing, and this is just—maybe this is just me and how I like to be communicated to—but I could just simply follow what he was trying to communicate. He had crisp questions… and I could just follow all of his questions, so I thought that was pretty effective. And I guess when it comes down to it at least to me, as a juror, I need to be able to follow the questions and the stream of thought in the case."*

Acquiring and retaining the jurors' attention is like hosting a holiday party. During the holiday season, many guests frequently have multiple gatherings to attend in a single night. How long a guest chooses to stay at each party depends on a variety of factors, including the type of music played, the kind of hors d'oeuvres served, the variety of people invited, and the nature of games played. Guests decline to attend or make excuses to leave parties they know will have dreadful music, horrid food, and unpleasant people. On the other hand, social gatherings that promise festive music, delightful beverages, scrumptious snacks, intriguing people, and amusing games entice guests and keep them there.

Just as the host of a party during the holiday season must vie for his guests' presence and time, the attorney must compete for the jurors' attention. It is crucial that the jury carefully listen to the evidence presented; an inattentive jury cannot possibly decide a case on a proper basis. Whether the jury grants the attorney its attention also depends on a variety of factors. The jury is much more likely to pay attention to an attorney who presents his case with enthusiasm and energy as opposed to with monotony and lethargy. Whether the attorney endeavors to make the trial interesting for the jurors also plays a role in whether the jurors focus intently on what he is saying. For instance, the jury will listen more attentively to attorneys who utilize engaging demonstratives than to ones who simply read from dull depositions.

• *Deliver on Your Promises*

It is essential that the jury trust us as attorneys. When the jurors do not trust us, they do not listen to us. If they do not listen to us, how are we going to persuade them of anything? Assertions made during opening statement set the stage for whether the jury perceives the attorney as sincere or as disingenuous. Throughout the remainder of trial, the jury observes carefully to see how the attorney's credibility plays out.

While making our opening statements, we need to (1) make realistic promises about what the evidence will show and (2) address facts harmful to our side of the case. During opening statement, the attorney's primary goal should be to persuade without overreaching. The attorney makes several promises to the jury during opening statement when he tells them what the evidence will show. The attorney should consult the jury charge to determine precisely what promises he should make. At the end of the trial, the jury has a series of questions to answer; therefore, the questions the jury will later be asked should dictate the attorney's promises.

We must avoid making promises that we cannot keep, especially concerning the facts and arguments related to the central issues in the case. Throughout the trial, the jury listens carefully for inconsistencies. If an attorney contradicts himself, whether blatant or subtle, the jury notices and holds the attorney accountable in some way.

> *"The defendant was, you know, pretty much catching all those—to me, if felt like he was catching all those lies and contradicting [the plaintiff's attorney]. And [the plaintiff's attorney] made himself contradict himself by saying certain things during the trial that made it sound like—okay, well, you just said earlier she was doing this, and when he showed the evidence, it showed us something different."*

By only making realistic promises during our openings, we ensure that we can deliver on all our promises during trial. Then, in closing, we have the opportunity to emphasize to the jury that we have proven everything that we guaranteed to them that we would. Making good on our promises goes a long way in solidifying our credibility.

While directing and crossing witnesses, we also should avoid making promises to the jury that we cannot keep. Toward the end of witness examinations, be careful when you use the phrase, "one more question." Although the attorney may find trivial the inconsistency between saying "last question" and his continuing to question the witness; to the jury, it is a broken promise. A small one, but a broken promise. And if you break promises—small or large—consistently, your credibility will suffer. We have never seen an attorney who has made this promise, fulfill it by asking only one more question. Inevitably, the attorney always asks more than one last question, thus undermining the attorney's credibility. When we fail to deliver on our promises, we as attorneys disappoint and frustrate the jury.

During opening statement, we must also address the thorns of our case. An attorney's failure to mention a negative fact that is clearly important to the lawsuit in no way prevents the jury from hearing it. In fact, when the jurors finally do learn of the obviously relevant albeit harmful evidence, they speculate as to the reason for the attorney's failure to disclose it. From the jurors' point of view, the attorney who omits crucial facts is (1) hiding something and (2) acting disingenuously. Declining to mention facts detrimental to our case also gives opposing counsel the ability to highlight our glaring omissions and to suggest that we had some sinister reason for failing to disclose important information to the jury.

Rule 4:
Set Expectations

Expectations are everything. How do you feel when someone tells you that he needs just a few minutes of your time and then 25 minutes later he is still talking to you? You feel misled, and your mind abandons whatever it is the offending speaker might be saying and turns to finding a graceful way to exit the conversation. Have you ever tried to hit a piñata blindfolded? It is both difficult and awkward as you cast about trying to locate the piñata. Both situations are not unlike the first-timer called down for jury service, thrown into a strange room with hundreds of other people and selected by number to go here and do this or that. The first-time juror has no idea how long his service will last, where the trip will end, or if he is doing things right. Part of our job as trial lawyers is to fix that.

It's not as if you can go down to the jury room and guide jurors from the minute they walk in the courthouse. But you can serve as a tour guide and leader the minute they step in the courtroom. In this chapter we will talk about things that you can do to help your jury understand what is going on, what to expect, and how long it will take. The benefit of these actions is that your jury will be better situated to focus. Instead of wondering, "What is this?" "Who is that?" "What is next?" and the ever important "Are we there yet?" jurors can focus on the facts of the case.

• *Set Reasonable Expectations Concerning Trial Length*

One of the most important issues to address for the jury is how long the trial will take. This matters on multiple levels, from whether the potential juror's schedule will allow her to participate to how long she expects to pay attention each day. Most jurors, especially those serving on jury duty for the first time, are unfamiliar with the legal system, other than through the television shows they watch each week. If those shows are to be believed, the entire case from the incident to closing argument can be handled in less than an hour. You have got to get this out of their heads and do so quickly. Ideally, the presiding judge confers with counsel and outlines for the jury the subject of the case, the anticipated time requirements for the trial, and the daily trial and break schedule.

Answering these questions for the jury is important; because if they are not answered, the jurors will be distracted the entire time wondering what happens next—when is lunch, or when do I get a bathroom break? None of these errant thoughts are helpful to your efforts to communicate with and persuade these jurors. Therefore, to the extent that the judge does not set expectations for the jury, you must fill that void and give them an itinerary for the trial.

As with any itinerary, your description should preview how long the trip will last and what the points of interest will be along the way. For example, during opening statement, the attorney might tell the jury: "Witness X will take approximately one hour, and I want you to listen for a particular question." I would also include a picture of that witness in your opening. By giving the jury a preview (with pictures), the attorney piques the jury's interest and focuses the jury's attention on the key issues of the trial.

Do not be afraid to keep telling the jury what is coming next. For example, each time I begin a new witness on direct, I start by asking the witness to introduce himself to the jury. Then I ask him why he is here or what he knows about this case. I do this to orient the jury in time and place. I want them to know who this witness is and how he fits in to the case. If I am lucky, one or two of the jurors may recall this witness from the picture that I used in opening and will be reminded of what I promised the witness would say about the case. Once the witness is done introducing himself and has been fit into the puzzle of the case, I say something to the effect of, "Mr. Jones, I would like to spend the next 45 minutes talking with you about your experience with X Corp." With this simple transition statement I have signaled the jury exactly how long this witness' testimony will last.

Jurors appreciate having someone set expectations for them. But there is an additional benefit that we have not discussed. When the expectations that you set prove correct, you build credibility with the jury. You are conditioning the jury to rely on what you tell them. They think, "If I can rely on him for how long a witness will last or what will happen next, then I can rely on him for what he says about the facts." The reverse is also true—if you fail to fulfill your promises and witnesses run on too long or you fail to produce the crucial piece of promised evidence, you will lose credibility in the eyes of the jury. They think, "If this lawyer can't even estimate how long it will take to present a witness, how am I supposed to trust him on the facts?"

For example, if you promise the jury that the trial will last three to four days and two weeks later you are still in trial, you have far overstayed your welcome and your request for their attention. And what happens when the in-laws stay too long? No one is happy; and everyone is tense, wondering "when will this end?" In the courtroom, the jury will become suspicious of the attorneys and view most, if not all, of their efforts as wasting time. The jury grows especially agitated when the lawyer who has exceeded the time limits repeats the same question again and again or requests multiple bench conferences. An irritated jury often punishes the attorney in some way. Therefore, create and keep realistic time promises.

Just keep in mind that the judge remains the king. The judge can disregard or negate anything that the attorney claims concerning how the trial will proceed. So before you start making promises about how the trial will proceed, be sure that you are not contradicting the judge or have the judge's approval to do so. I once saw this backfire in the jury selection process. The judge specifically instructed counsel not to tell anyone how long the trial was going to last. She was concerned that the length of the trial would unearth an unnecessary number of hardship claims. Despite that admonition, my opposing counsel barreled straight ahead, telling the jury that the trial would last three weeks and asked if that would be a problem for anyone. The judge immediately reprimanded the attorney and corrected him in front of the jury. This did little for the attorney's credibility with the judge and made him look foolish in front of the jury. To avoid stepping on the judge's toes and looking amateurish before the jury, make sure you have the court's approval prior to commenting on how the trial will proceed.

Sometimes, it may be necessary to "de-set" expectations. Jurors all bring certain life experiences into the courtroom. One of the biggest expectations that we have to deal with as attorneys is what jurors see on T.V. Between *CSI, Law and Order* and all those darn T.V. lawyer shows, most jurors think every lawyer has an investigative team of detectives and forensic experts. We don't. But if you ever have a case where something like that could have been used in the evidentiary process, the jury will expect to see it. And more damaging, if they do not see it, they will assume that it is because you did not have the evidence. If you did not have the evidence then your case must not be very good.

"Because we're all so in tune with **Law and Order** *and* **CSI**, *on the criminal case, of course everyone wanted DNA, which of course didn't exist, which they told us right from the beginning—'Okay, you're all going to want DNA, but this isn't television.'"*

Clearly, the lawyers should have done some "de-setting" of expectations here. When thinking about your next trial, think if there is anything about the television lawyer shows that might have set up an expectation you need to either meet or debunk. Most jurors have been exposed to legal novels, movies, and television shows. Although the jury probably realizes what they have seen or read is mere fiction, popular media still plays a part in dictating the jury's expectations concerning trial proceedings. At the outset of the case, the lawyer should address what predispositions the jury is likely to have to avoid disappointing the jury.

• *Set Time Limits*

In every case, the attorney faces two competing interests. On the one hand, you have to respect and not waste your jurors' time. The best way to accomplish this is to present the case quickly and expediently. On the other hand, you must present and respond to all of the evidence in support of your client's case. One of the techniques we use to accomplish this is a self-imposed time budget. We would prefer that all judges put us on time limits. Attorneys generally spend way too long presenting their cases, but most judges are reluctant to manage a trial quite this aggressively without good reason. By imposing a time budget, you force yourself to make decisions about the priority of your evidence. Let's face it, there is a limited amount of time that anyone wants to listen to an economic expert talk about damages or a human factors expert talk about the interactions of the human nervous system. Just like your household budget or childhood allowance, you have to make decisions about how you will allocate your precious dollars. During trial, your precious resource is time in front of the jury. You have to decide exactly how much of the time before the jury should be used with a given witness. We find this technique helps us balance between the two competing interests. Jurors like to feel that their time is being used efficiently, and therefore greatly appreciate the attorney who imposes and sticks to time limits. Time constraints also prove advantageous to the client because they force the attorney to prioritize the evidence and decide what is essential and what is expendable, ensuring that the attorney presents the best case possible.

Time limits compel the attorney to take a much harder look at the evidence than he would otherwise and force her to separate the essential wheat of the evidence from the unnecessary chaff. Time constraints force attorneys to budget their time well. When the attorney only has a certain amount of time to examine witnesses, he allows more time for crucial witnesses, leaving less time for peripheral witnesses. Having a time constraint ensures that the attorney cuts out the fat of the case and focuses solely on the meat. In other words, the attorney streamlines the case. By streamlining the case, the attorney encourages the jury to focus on the true disputes of the case as opposed to extraneous facts.

Attorneys have a difficult time knowing when to rest their cases, and time limits ensure that the trial is finite. A trial attorney is rarely content with the case he has put on. In each trial, the attorney feels he could have put on several more witnesses and admitted many additional documents. Because the attorney can always admit more documents, call more witnesses, and ask more questions, a trial can literally take three days, three weeks, or three months. How long a trial lasts often depends on how much time the judge allots to each party. Of course, in criminal cases, time limits may not be an option. Due process requires that the criminal defendant have the opportunity to put forth as much evidence as he desires. Therefore, if the criminal defendant wishes to admit additional evidence and question additional witnesses, the judge cannot prevent him from doing so. However, in civil cases, the judge has nearly absolute discretion with respect to how much time each side gets to present his case. Even if the judge chooses not to allot to each side a certain amount of time, the attorney should volunteer to impose time constraints on himself. To keep himself accountable, the attorney should inform the judge and the jury of how long he anticipates his side of the case will take.

I liken setting time limits to Odysseus' binding himself to the mast in the epic poem, *The Odyssey*. The hero Odysseus faces a challenge. He must pass by islands inhabited by Sirens, seductresses who lure sailors with enchanting music to crash their ships on rocks and cliffs. Prior to passing the Sirens' isles, Odysseus instructs the members of his crew to put beeswax into their ears so that the seductresses will not tempt them. Odysseus longed to listen to the song of the Sirens but knew that if he did, he would inevitably run his ship into the cliffs. Odysseus therefore bade his men tie him to the mast of the ship. Being bound to the mast enabled Odysseus to hear the song of the Sirens while avoiding the inexorable temptation to crash his vessel.

Left untied, Odysseus would have been unable to prevent himself from crashing his ship into the cliffs. Likewise, left to our own devices, lawyers cannot keep themselves from going on and on and on with the presentation of evidence in a trial. Just as Odysseus bound himself to the ship to stop himself from succumbing to the temptation to run his ship into the rocks, we must set time constraints to prevent ourselves from doing something that perhaps we cannot do of our own free will—bring the case to an end and close our evidence.

• *Renegotiate Commitments When Necessary*

Does this mean that we have never missed a commitment at anytime ever in court? No. We are human. We have under/overestimated time, and circumstances beyond our control have pushed us beyond trial lengths we once thought were valid. So what do you do then? I steal a page from the playbook of David Allen and his wonderful book *Getting Things Done*. We recommend it to every attorney. In the book, Allen discusses the importance of time management. He likens life to a series of commitments. Our goal is to keep every commitment that we make. But there are times in life that we just can't keep every commitment that we made. So what does Allen recommend? He recommends that you renegotiate and get an extension. Allen explains that every commitment—whether the commitment is to one's self, one's spouse, one's boss, or one's client—can be renegotiated. Lunch dates can be moved to a later date and meetings can be postponed. Although commitments can be renegotiated, they cannot be simply ignored without consequence. Why should the jury be any different?

The attorney should treat commitments he makes to the jury just as he would treat any other commitment. If something unexpected transpires causing the trial to extend further than the attorney had stated it would, he should identify the extenuating circumstances and reset expectations. Is this ideal? No, but it is better than just blowing your commitment without explanation. As soon as you realize that the trial will take longer to try than originally promised, let the jury know. Tell them what happened and how much time will be added to your original promise. Or, if you do not yet know, tell them exactly what is going on. For example, you might say, "This next witness was a last minute addition; and until we get through with this testimony, we cannot tell you specifically when the trial will end. But as soon as we are done with this witness, we will get back to you."

Think about flying on a plane. I much prefer the chatty pilot to the one who says nothing. Don't you like the pilot who comes on and says, "We have a great route, and I am going to be able to make up some time for you." Or how about the pilot who comes on and tells me, "We have had to vector around some weather to keep us safe. The flight is going to be 20 minutes longer, but you will be safe." I may not be thrilled about the delay, but I am definitely in favor of being safe. The pilot has reset my expectations, and I can go back to what I am doing on the flight, confident we are in the hands of a professional.

The jury understands that sometimes the ball bounces funny, and we have to react to it. If a trial extends longer than you predicted and you explain what happened and ask for an extension, the jury will not hold it against you because you have been straightforward with them. On the other hand, if the trial takes longer than the jury expected and the attorney does not make a point of renegotiating his commitment with the jury, the jury will hold it against the attorney, negatively affecting the client.

One more point before we leave this issue. Juries are just like judges. One request for extension is acceptable. Two is pushing it, but ok. If you make a third, fourth or fifth request for an extension, be prepared to face a skeptical and untrusting audience from there on out. You can seek an extension, but be judicious in your requests.

• *Give Clear Direction Via Roadmaps, or Other Devices*

Americans rarely venture too far from home without a map, GPS, or some navigational system. Prior to taking road trips, people either get out a roadmap or visit Google Maps to determine the best route. Just as atlases prove indispensable to people in reaching their intended destinations across the globe, "roadmaps" and other tools also prove essential to jurors in navigating through a case.

Giving the jury an overview of where the case will go before you jump into the minutia will prove beneficial to both you and your jury. The roadmap is an efficient way to inform the jury what is going to take place in trial. A roadmap consists of a few sentences that tell the jury where the case is going generally. The attorney succinctly states the major disputes and what the evidence will show. By giving the jury a roadmap at the start of the trial, the attorney provides the jury with a good overall picture of the facts and issues so that they can better traverse the case. A roadmap at the beginning of the case signals to the jury where the case is going. Then, throughout the trial, the attorney can revisit the roadmap to remind the jury where they are in the journey. The purpose of the roadmap is to make it easy for the jury to understand where you are going and how you intend to get there.

While we are on the subject of making things easy on the jury, let's spend a few minutes on how to package evidence for the jury. Our job is to make the final decision as easy as possible for the jury. That means that if you have a case with a lot of documents that added together make up your damages or you need to connect the dots between many documents, don't just leave that for the jury to do. Package your case in such a way that it will be easy for the jury to access the information. Let's take a look at what one juror in a medical malpractice case said about his efforts to compile and decipher medical bills in the record.

> *"We had some medical bills and [the plaintiff] said, 'Oh yeah, my son had all these medical bills.' But it was hard for us because we had stacks and stacks of papers with just numbers, so it was really hard for us to go through and match things up. You don't want to not do it but at the same time it really leads people to say, 'Oh well, this is almost too much effort to try to go through all this.' If you can make the evidence really concise and understandable—point it out to us, 'Okay, this is exactly what's going on and this is why.'"*

On an issue as important as damages, why would any attorney want to make the jury work this hard to understand his case and potentially be unable to complete the verdict form? The attorney should avoid giving the jury an unmanageable load of documents. However, in some cases, we have no choice but to admit numerous documents for the jury to examine. Understandably, meticulously inspecting lots of documents proves tiresome and tedious to the jury. Attorneys need to provide the jurors with a compass so that they can find their way through the forest of documents. The jury's job description does not include searching through a haystack of evidence to find a particular needle. The attorney should not demand that the jury rifle through evidence to locate something the attorney mentions during trial. Rather, the attorney needs to make the evidence he relies on readily available to the jury.

One of the most important road maps is your closing argument. I'm a strong believer in the statement, "If you cannot or do not say it to the jury, you cannot expect them to say it back to you." So it is imperative that you ask the jury for the result that you want. Notice that we are saying "ask." Do not demand action from the jury or even tell them what to do. Instead tell them, "Based on the evidence, we are requesting that you answer this question "yes" or "no" or "$1,500,000." Make clear to them what you are requesting that they do. Otherwise, the jurors are left to guess how much to award, and there is literally no telling what they will come up with. Read what one juror had to say on this very subject.

"You have to award money and some of the attorneys did not place an amount. And so we . . . when we were back deliberating, it was like what amount do we start with? And it's just kind of like somebody threw out an amount, and we kind of went, okay. So even though you can't put a, you know, a price on life but we have to and so I think it was helpful whenever the attorneys did put an amount there."

Could the struggle be any clearer? Without direction and guidance from the attorneys, the jury finds it difficult to determine what to put in the jury questionnaire. Again, this is the last thing that we want. We want to make the evidence and the case as easy and accessible for the jurors as possible. Not suggesting to the jury particular amounts for damages is like asking the jury to take a shot in the dark—it is simply not effective. The jury needs for the attorney to give them guidance with respect to how much money to award.

To summarize the importance of roadmaps, rather than leave the jurors to fend for themselves in reaching decisions about the case, the attorney should provide the jury with direction. At the outset of the case, the attorney should give the jury a roadmap so that they have a general idea of where the trial is going. Throughout the trial, the attorney should use signaling principles to reiterate the route he has created for the jury. The attorney should also direct the jury to the pieces of evidence he relies on and wants the jury to focus on. By giving the jury all of the necessary tools, the attorney helps the jury stay true to the path and prevents them from getting lost in a forest of irrelevant details.

• *Avoid Saying "One More Question"*

As we mentioned in *Rule 3: Be Credible*, lawyers frequently state "one more question" or "last question" toward the end of their examination of a witness or when the judge asks if the lawyer has further questions. Between the ninety or so trials that we [Trey Cox and James Stanton] have tried together, not a single attorney who has claimed "last question" has actually asked the witness only one more question. Because inevitably the attorney will always ask more than one last question, making such statements hurts the attorney's credibility. Also, using such phrases serves literally no purpose. The judge will never force an attorney to tell him beforehand the precise number of inquiries he plans to make, and volunteering a specific number in no way benefits the attorney or his client.

By telling the jury "final question," the attorney sets the jurors expectations. When the attorney proceeds to ask multiple questions as opposed to just one more after making such a statement, the attorney impugns his credibility with the jury. The jury finds that the attorney has failed as a steward of their time and simply stops listening to the attorney's line of questioning.

The attorney should ask himself why he feels compelled to make the commitment of asking "one last question" and what the statement suggests to the judge and to the jury. Perhaps the attorney realizes that he has foregone the jury's focus by taking far too long on one witness and by stating "final question," is seeking to regain the jury's attention.

When the judge asks you whether you would like to ask further questions of a witness, you should simply reply "yes"—this is the case even if you truly intend to ask only a single question. By responding to the judge "yes" or "yes, just a few," you maintain control of the examination as opposed to ceding it to the witness. When you question an adverse witness and tell the judge "one more question" or state to the witness "final question," the witness often does everything in his power to ensure that his responses necessitate that you ask him numerous questions as opposed to just one.

• *Make Jurors Comfortable*

The attorney should set the potential jurors' expectations concerning how they will be treated during voir dire and during trial. During voir dire, the judge typically informs the venire that if anyone feels uncomfortable answering private questions in front of the others, he may approach the bench for an individual conversation with the judge. Should the judge fail to tell the venire this, the attorney should do so. The purpose of apprising the potential jurors of the option to privately converse with the judge is to make them feel comfortable; therefore, the attorney should make the bench seem safe. The attorney should make it clear that should a potential juror desire an individual exchange with the judge, the judge will not rake the potential juror over the coals by interrogating him but rather will treat him with respect.

Even after the jurors have been selected, the attorney should continue his endeavors to make jurors feel at ease. Jurors appreciate the attorney who recognizes that jurors have lives outside of the courtroom and who attempts to make the trial as pleasant as possible for the jurors. The attorney should always be considerate of the jury as the jury ultimately holds the client's fate in its hands. The considerate lawyer tries a concise, to-the-point case and does not prolong the trial unnecessarily.

Rule 5:
Be Sincere

Jurors expect lawyers to believe in their client's case. Our jurors told us that they felt like some lawyers were just going through the motions or did not display the dedication to the client's cause the way the jurors expected. The American author and humorist, Garrison Keillor, talks about the importance of passion in motivating your audience: "You taught me to be nice, so nice that now I am so full of niceness, I have no sense of right and wrong, no outrage, no passion." As we discussed in *Rule 1: Respect The Process*, jurors want to feel they are being motivated to do the right and just thing. The passionless advocate disappoints them.

Other jurors told us they were unpersuaded when lawyers made emotional arguments that did not pertain to the case. Specifically, some lawyers were outraged at inappropriate times or suggested that the jury should make their decision based on the bad economy. These jurors echoed the thoughts of English novelist and literary critic David Lawrence who talked about the importance of genuine passion: "Be still when you have nothing to say; when genuine passion moves you, say what you've got to say, and say it hot." This genuine, hot passion to reach the just result is what jurors are desperately seeking.

> *"Being an attorney isn't a whole lot different than being a salesman, in that you're basically selling your side of the story. And with doing that, you need to come off sincere. You need to come off caring."*

Whereas an overabundance of passion coupled with a shortage of logic may hurt a lawyer's credibility, feigned emotion destroys it. Although jurors may not be particularly well versed in the law, they are extraordinarily adept at judging whether someone acts genuinely or not. The jury knows whether an attorney honestly believes in his client, his cause, and his case or whether the attorney is merely putting on a show in order to manipulate them.

> *"And there was some of that stereotypical sleazy lawyer stuff,*
> *I hate to say. But I did feel that those attorneys were trying to*
> *manipulate me a little bit, and I felt I was able to see through*
> *that pretty easily."*

Jurors are experts in human behavior—they have dealt with people every single day since birth. As experts in reading people, jurors essentially comprise a corporate lie detector test. Though they may be clever, attorneys are not immune from the jury's expertise in distinguishing lies from the truth. The jury's ability to discern genuineness reaches even to an attorney's cunning tricks and charming persuasions. Jurors can easily tell the difference between a truthful witness and a dishonest witness, and they can just as readily discern between a sincere attorney and a disingenuous one. Jurors undoubtedly notice when an attorney endeavors to manipulate them and they strongly resent it. Hence, sincerity is essential to trying a case.

• *Believe in Your Case Intellectually*

Passion alone goes only so far with the jury. To be an effective advocate, the lawyer must do more than appeal to the jury's emotions—he must articulate why his side wins the case based on logic. Realistically, only cases in which liability is uncertain go to trial. Clear-cut cases in which one party is unquestionably in the right and the other undoubtedly in the wrong almost always settle. Jurors' gut responses to close-call cases will vary; therefore, making a passionate, emotional appeal to the jury is not enough.

The attorney must meticulously address all of the evidence in the case, including facts disadvantageous to the attorney's side. The best way to handle negative evidence is to incorporate it into the trial alongside evidence favorable to your side of the case. Taking the evidence as a whole, you can then explain why your side wins the trial based on underlying logic.

• *Pay Attention to Your Audience to Gauge Their Reaction*

In a game of golf, the successful player concentrates on the ground, the ball, and the club. Golf does not require that players mingle with the sport's spectators. In fact, the very structure of the game discourages players from interacting with observers in the midst of the game. In order to do well, golf requires that the players look down and focus solely on accurately hitting the ball. The game's observers play absolutely no role in the game. Whether the spectators respect the golfer or loathe him in no way affects the game's end result.

Trial advocacy is nothing like a golf game. When litigating a trial, much of the attorney's attention should be on the jurors, who serve not only as the trial's observers but also as its decision-makers. The attorney must meaningfully interact with the jury, because whether the jury finds the attorney credible seriously impacts the outcome of the case. To succeed in the game of trial litigation, you need to gain the trust of the jurors. Jurors, like the rest of American society, highly value eye contact and deem those individuals who avoid it as dishonest and disingenuous. Therefore, in order to build credibility and rapport with the jury, look up from your notes and make eye contact with each juror.

Keeping your head up during trial not only enables you to meaningfully interact with the jurors by making eye contact with them, but it also gives you the opportunity to observe the jury, see how they are responding, and react accordingly.

"Number one, if you get a chance, glance at your jury, see how your jury is responding to you. If your jury is—I wouldn't say stone-faced but if they look as if they're disinterested—then you may need to change your routine some kind of way. And if you look over at your jury and you see some faces in which you look as if you're annoying them, whatever it is, stop doing it. And especially the air quotes—I hate them. And we had an attorney who was doing that. And it annoyed the hell out of us jurors. As soon as we got back to the jury room, we were all screaming that if we could come out of the jury box, we would grab his hands and tape them to his side. We were like please, don't do that. Air quotes, no, out."

Make a point of attending to the jury and noting how they are reacting. Otherwise, you will be oblivious to the jury's distraction or irritation at your method of presenting the case. Be flexible in your style of advocacy. If you recognize that the jury is not reacting well to your manner of arguing the case, adapt accordingly. For example, if the jury appears bored and disinterested, try to communicate the case in a more entertaining fashion to recapture the jury's attention. Likewise, make an effort to be conscious of your mannerisms; if they appear to agitate the jury, stop immediately. A lawyer's bad habits may seem inconsequential; however, they are not trivial when they divert the jury's attention from the case at hand.

• *Treat the Case as More Than Just a Job*

Jurors want to feel the lawyer picked her client and her client's case because the client is in the right not because the case was profitable. Or worse yet, the jury should never get the impression that the attorney is working on the loser case out of a sense of obligation or inability to say "no."

"Just try to be sincere. Try to really bring across that you believe this to be the right thing. Because if you're just hired to do a job and you present a bunch of evidence but you don't even know exactly what it is yourself, then it's very difficult for the jury to understand it, too."

A lawyer should have two goals during every trial: to clearly communicate the theme of the case to the jury and to establish himself as credible. In crafting and communicating the theme, the lawyer needs to realize that jurors will not understand every legal concept that he delves into. You simply cannot expect a lay jury to appreciate the finer distinctions of the law. Despite your best intentions, the lay jury will never grasp every legal nuance of the case—whether it be negligence, securities fraud, or medical malpractice. Attempting to explain legal nuances to the jury either wastes time because it goes over the jurors' heads, or it proves detrimental to the case because the jurors misinterpret the law.

Although jurors lack familiarity with the law, they are smart about people because they interact with them daily and in every aspect of their lives. Due to their vast experience with humankind, the jury can readily discern when a person is being truthful and when they are telling a falsehood. The factfinders therefore feel insulted when attorneys attempt to instruct them how to tell when a witness is lying—this is a determination the jury has been making since childhood. Once the attorney gives the jury the dots, he has done his job. The jury is well qualified to connect the dots and will resist an attorney who tries to handhold them. Your time is far better spent drawing the jury's attention to reasons a witness might have a motive to be untruthful than purporting to teach the jury how to distinguish the truth from a lie.

• *Passionate Argument v. Arguing Passionately*

To effectively communicate a case to the jury, formulate a trial strategy based on sound logic. Juries are far more amenable to considering arguments founded in reason than they are to considering emotional appeals and rants about injustice. This is not to say that the attorney should argue the case dryly or dispassionately. Once you've organized your case around reason, you should deliver your logical argument with fervor.

"Given the circumstances of the case, I think it could have been probably portrayed more dramatically than it was. And I didn't know if that was intentional because maybe they didn't want to come across as so over the top that the jury gets turned off because they're putting on a big show or something. But on the other hand, my lord, this is this woman's son, and it was very tragic and traumatic of an accident. I mean, to be hit at 65 miles an hour by a medical van, you know, when you're walking. I mean, that is extremely traumatic, and yet I don't know that it was probably portrayed as emotionally from the plaintiff's perspective as it could have been."

Under certain circumstances, the jury expects you to be passionate about the case. Not being emotional when the jury anticipates it can be distracting. Also, dispassionate attorneys come across to juries as callous, uncaring, and as though they are merely there to do a job. On the other hand, a lawyer who argues the case enthusiastically captures the jury's attention.

> *"He was very vibrant, very loud, very energetic. The other was very quiet, completely the opposite. One kept us awake. And like I said, he brought a lot of character to his side of the case. The other tried to mirror that, but didn't quite catch it."*

• *Believe in Your Client*

Whether the attorney is confident in the client's case makes an immense difference to the jury. Many juries are of the mindset that if the attorney does not believe in his own client, why should they? Also, jurors tend to discredit lawyers who defend clients in whom they lack confidence.

> *"I think believe in your client. If you truly believe that your client is innocent, then you can defend him. If you don't believe your client is innocent, I don't think you should defend him."*

There are a variety of ways a lawyer can express his belief in his client to the jury. Of course, how you express this belief depends on what comes naturally to you. Al Ellis, a personal injury attorney who practices in Dallas, serves as an excellent example of how to show a jury that you believe in your client. After examining a witness, Ellis approaches and puts his arm around his client. He asks whether the client would like him to ask any additional questions and whether the client is content with the examination. By putting his arm around his client, Ellis shows that he cares about and is concerned for his client's well-being. And by asking whether his client is happy with the questioning, Ellis shows that he trusts his client and values his client's opinion.

The need for attorneys to express belief in their clients is fairly self-evident in the personal injury context; however, it may prove advantageous in all areas of the law. For example, when a corporation is a party to a case, showing that you have faith in the person in charge of the corporation not only adds credibility to the corporate client but also aids in the necessary personalization of the corporation.

• *Ensure that Your Client Is Present, Passionate, and Personable*

By ensuring that your client is present, passionate, and personable, you encourage the jury to empathize with your client and to believe in your side of the case. Juries want to see trial participants who truly seem to care about the outcomes of their cases. Genuine human emotion piques and keeps the jury's interest.

Jurors naturally sympathize with human beings but have a fairly difficult time relating to corporate entities, so personalizing corporate clients is crucial to arguing the case. How a CEO should address a crisis situation proves analogous to how a lawyer should handle a corporate client during trial. During a corporate crisis, the CEO must personalize the corporation by publicly serving as the face of the company and being knowledgeable enough about both the corporation and the crisis to intelligently respond to any inquiries.

Likewise, when representing a corporate client, the attorney must humanize the corporation. An attorney humanizes a corporate client by designating one person to act as the face of the corporation. That person must be present for the entirety of the trial—otherwise, the company appears flippant and unconcerned about the case. The person chosen to serve as the face of the corporation must be personable and human. Additionally, that person must be knowledgeable about the subject matter of the case and not constantly having to refer to someone else for answers during trial.

• *Drama, Theater, Entertainment*

> *"The courtroom is really a theater and there are players, and they have their roles."*

Jurors have grown accustomed to watching *CSI, Law and Order, Boston Legal,* and a litany of other legal television shows. Due in part to these popular legal dramas, jurors anticipate that they will be told a story, and they expect to be entertained. Attorneys should not disappoint the jury in this regard. When presenting the case, the attorney should keep in mind that most jurors are visual learners who absorb information more readily by seeing demonstratives than by hearing spoken words. We will go into this in more detail in *Rule 9* on the use of demonstrative evidence. But for purposes of this rule, it is important to point out that you are more likely to strike a chord of emotion with the jurors if you involve them in a storyline that they both hear and see.

> *"What they should have had was an overhead visual of the facility where the accident occurred and then moveable objects to represent the truck and people so that they could position everything without writing it here and we're scratching it out."*

Giving an oral explanation of what transpired is unlikely to hold the jury's attention. Visuals are far more interesting and therefore more effective than spoken words. For example, if the case involves an automobile accident, presenting a demonstrative that sets the stage of the accident and has moving parts that recreate what happened proves immensely helpful to the jury in understanding how the accident took place. These kinds of demonstrations create a powerful marriage of logic and emotion.

Jurors recognize that much of a trial is scripted and that just as directors rehearse with their actors, so attorneys rehearse with and "woodshed" their clients. Jurors appreciate good acting not only in the theater but also in the courtroom.

"The biggest thing that I remember about the attorneys or the lawyers was the way they both decided to carry themselves. The one that stands out the most is the plaintiff's attorney spent a lot of time trying to be too folksy. We know you're well-educated... It was unfortunate that some of the jurors really felt like why is he doing this? We want educated people trying these cases—why can't you do that?"

"Those closing arguments, there was a lot of fist pounding and drama. And in my face. We all kind of laughed, the jurors, because we had an experience where the lawyer—the attorney for the defense was so close to us and he was pounding his fist and spitting. And I was Juror Number 2 in the front, so instead of listening to him, I was kind of backing up because I was actually getting wet."

Although jurors are well aware of the attorney's bias toward his client and his goal of exacting the most favorable reaction from the jury, each juror is willing to suspend his disbelief in order to truly get into the story. However, the jury cannot do this unless the attorney appears to act naturally. The jury wishes to be entertained—they do not wish to be manipulated by an attorney's feigning a personality he believes will appeal to them. The attorney needs to be entertaining while still being his true self.

• *Build the Case around the Jury Charge*

In jury trials, each case ultimately boils down to the judge's legal determinations throughout the trial and the jury's responses to factual questions in the jury charge. Attorneys should therefore frame their arguments to fit within the law and then argue the factual issues which the jury decides. More specifically, the attorney should structure the case to mirror the jury charge. Prior to deliberations in every case, the judge will instruct the jury: "You are the sole judges of the credibility of the witnesses and the weight to be given their testimony." Bearing this in mind, the attorney should alert the jury when he presents factual arguments as these—fact issues lie solely within their discretion.

Unfortunately, many lawyers spend an inordinate amount of time arguing about things which, under the law, the jury cannot decide. This not only wastes time but it also distracts the jury from the issues that they will actually resolve. Leading juries to believe that they will be deciding matters within the discretion of the judge confuses the jury and causes them to consider inappropriate issues during deliberations; similarly, failing to teach the jury how your facts apply to the legal definitions in the jury charge can harm your case.

"Most of this came down to the first question of was there negligence in this case. And what was interesting was it was never really brought up by the lawyers during voir dire, during the opening and closing arguments: did you think the case itself, any discussion about or arguments for was there negligence, was there not negligence, here's the legal definition of negligence. Here's why we believe that you should find for our client or not for our client. It was never really anything proposed to us by the lawyers, and so we were left as a jury to sort of say, 'We saw the facts in this case. We've been provided a legal definition, and we had to make a determination from there.' The lawyers never really argued on that one point which seemed to me to be the most important point of all."

Rather than simply stating the facts and leaving the jury to their own devices to ascertain what to make of the evidence, the attorney should provide the jury with some direction. The attorney directs the jury by organizing the case around the questions the jury will answer and by clearly articulating the points he wants to get across throughout the trial. This aids the jury during their deliberations by keeping them focused on the issues they will decide.

> *"Like one of the witnesses, they did a good job of getting information out of her or at least they got the information they wanted to. But then in my mind, it was all jumbled. It wasn't like this is the information you got, this is why it's good, this is why it helps the plaintiff. It was like a whole bunch of information. I don't know which one you want me to know or emphasize or anything like that. It was just there."*

The attorney should consider the jury charge at all levels of the case. The jury charge should influence the content of the opening statement as well as closing argument. Additionally, the attorney should consider the charge while directing and crossing witnesses. The attorney should structure the direct examinations and the cross examinations in a way that clearly expresses to the jury what the attorney wants the jury to know as opposed to asking a series of disorganized questions and leaving the jury to guess what they were supposed to glean from witnesses' testimony.

• *A Word of Caution: Too Much Passion Hurts Your Credibility*

Jurors typically believe that emotion may play no role in their deliberations, a fact which provides an additional reason for attorneys to focus on arguing logic to the jury as opposed to appealing to the jury's sympathies. Prior to deliberations in every case, the judge instructs the jury according to the Texas Rules of Civil Procedure: "Do not let bias, prejudice or sympathy play any part in your deliberations." Many attorneys harp on this language during closing argument, reminding jurors to only consider the evidence presented during trial when reaching a decision. Although the instruction does not tell juries to disassociate themselves from emotion when reaching a factual conclusion, juries often interpret the instruction to mean that emotion may play no part in their deliberations.

> *"You know, as a juror, you're just supposed to deal with the facts and not get emotionally involved either way."*

> *"I'm an emotional person and I'm a very empathetic person, so*
> *I was telling myself as I was watching this individual cry, I had*
> *to allow myself that empathy but I had to put that aside when*
> *it comes time to make a decision."*

Jurors equate passion with emotion and therefore consciously avoid allowing an attorney's passion for the case to affect their deliberations. When presenting factual arguments, the attorney should convey to the jury that they are encouraged to use their emotions when making factual decisions. If advantageous to his side of the case in any particular trial, the lawyer should clear up this prevalent misconception concerning the jury instruction. For instance, the plaintiff in a personal injury case may want to encourage the jury to invoke their emotions when deliberating whereas the defendant in the same case would simply tell the jury to avoid sympathy and focus solely on the facts. Lawyers should educate jurists that the instruction regarding bias, sympathy, and prejudice does not prohibit them from being passionate and emotional about the case. The instruction simply means that the jury may not let sympathy and bias take over the deliberation process.

Because jurors tend to believe that they are prohibited from letting their emotions influence their decisions, jurors seek a non-emotional basis on which to decide the case. Even jurors who allow sentiment to factor into their deliberations are not comfortable reaching a conclusion based wholly on their feelings. Therefore, arguing the case based primarily on passion will undoubtedly prove ineffective.

> *"We're here to listen to the facts not the drama."*

Considering that juries are under the impression that they must ban emotion from their deliberations, playing solely on the jury's emotions proves unhelpful. Because the jury makes an effort to reach an objective decision, they are likely to consciously put aside any emotional response they may have to the case and concentrate on the objective facts.

Emotionally, jurors may want to decide in a particular direction, but they will avoid that decision unless there is a logical/factual case to hang their hat on.

> *"What I really thought was effective that the attorneys did was very methodically step-by-step led us through the series of events that we were all where we were. What I didn't like was the attorney who thought he could just get us emotionally against the plaintiff just because of the current situation and economics and make it about David and Goliath rather than the methodical facts. He didn't have any facts and so I think he was just trying to use pure emotion which isn't as effective."*

The appeal to emotion should be subtle not direct. Rather than focusing on invoking a sentimental reaction from the jury, the lawyer should present the jury with logical reasons for why his side wins the case. Where juries can articulate the underlying logic and factual basis of their decisions, they have no qualms reaching an emotionally pleasing decision.

Rule 6:
Be Transparent

• *The Giver of Truth*

We best serve our client when we deliver our case to the jury with an attitude of transparency and authenticity. In this context, transparency means conveying the facts to the jury straightforwardly and genuinely, and never leaving a juror wondering, "What am I missing? What are they trying to hide from me?"

Too often trial attorneys take the stage with the view that they are the lead actor in the production; yet, if we were using a theatrical metaphor, we would do better to think of ourselves as the narrator. Traditionally, the narrator functions as a conduit of information. The narrator is unaffected by the outcome of the story; therefore, the narrator is in a position to impartially relay the facts to an audience. Because the narrator remains neutral while telling the story, the audience does not suspect the narrator of taking the side of any character but rather wholeheartedly believes in the accuracy of the narrator's recitation of the facts.

Similarly, in a trial, the attorney serves primarily as a conveyor of facts. Like the narrator, the attorney has no role in the actual story underlying the trial. Rather, the attorney's role is to organize and communicate the story to the jurors. The attorney avoids detracting from the story of his case by remaining as inconspicuous as possible and endeavoring never to intrude upon the story.

Unlike the narrator, the attorney is in no position to relay the facts in an entirely disinterested fashion. The jury understands we are paid to represent our clients. Whereas the reader never suspects the narrator would favor a particular character in the story, the jury is under no illusion that the attorney slants facts in favor of his client. Although the jury understands that the lawyer is a hired gun, the attorney can maintain credibility with the jury by keeping the jury's focus on the case as opposed to drawing the jury's attention to himself.

The narrator is the guide. He takes the listeners by the hand and guides them through the facts and events of the story to the very end. Your job as the trial narrator is to determine how the story will be told in terms of structure or witness order and which facts are the most relevant, and most importantly, at the end of the day, to suggest what conclusions can be drawn from the facts and events.

Narrators don't have to tell the truth. They can tell the truth as they see it, as an unbiased witness to the events of the story. They can tell the truth as they perceive it, which means interpreting events to support a personal truth. Just because a narrator is telling the story doesn't mean he or she is telling the true or entire story.

To most effectively tell the story of the case, we must act as an honest, transparent broker of information. By straightforwardly relaying the facts during trial, we appear impartial and begin to build credibility. The less blatantly biased the attorney appears, the more credible the jury finds the attorney.

• *Ensure Witnesses Are Transparent*

Jurors also expect witnesses to serve as transparent conveyors of fact. To jurors, a transparent witness is one who simply reports the facts. Juries become suspicious of witnesses who overact or equivocate. Often the most convincing witness does not share a close relationship with any party and does not have a direct interest in the outcome of the case. Here is what one juror told us about the value of a disinterested third-party witness:

> *"Well the most credible witness we saw was the one that was the most removed from it. He had come in just to do an inspection of the house. He didn't know either party. He knew a few of the people in construction but not really personally— they weren't his friends or anything. He knew them as work acquaintances. He was the most fair. He just told us strictly what was wrong with the house, what the basics were, whether or not he could tell if it was new or old. And he was really the most credible witness we saw. And I think it was because he was so far removed from the actual situation."*

Expert witnesses, especially those who are not retained specifically for the case, are very persuasive because they are the furthest removed from the case. Jurors realize that although expert witnesses are often paid to testify, they have no real stake in the controversy. When selecting fact witnesses, keep in mind that jurors often lock onto and believe testimony from a witness lacking a dog in the fight. Inevitably, many necessary witnesses have biases that are self-evident to the jury. Fortunately, the jury understands human relationships, loyalties, and motives. The jury knows that the testimony of a mother is likely to favor her son, the testimony of a best friend will probably support his buddy, and the testimony of a well-paid employee will probably prefer his boss. The lawyer minimizes these common biases by encouraging his witnesses to straightforwardly respond to the questions asked of them. Regardless of the relationship, the jurors will observe each witness and evaluate body language. If a witness stammers or stutters or seems unsure of himself, the jury will naturally question the witness's credibility. Similarly, if a witness exaggerates or talks in circles to avoid difficult questions, jurors also will question his credibility. Here is what one juror had to say about witness body language and mannerisms.

> *"The defendant's testimony was believable, and the person who said she was assaulted was not believable at all. Her story didn't make sense, and we all agreed, and it took a very short time to say this is bogus—he didn't do anything. She stammered and kind of talked in circles and didn't answer the questions directly, and she embellished and added stuff that was irrelevant in a lot of cases and made it more dramatic-sounding. And he just told the facts very straightforwardly."*

Straightforward witnesses are simply more compelling than overly dramatic ones. Witnesses who exaggerate draw the jury away from the central story and detract from the case. By appearing transparent, the witness creates and maintains credibility with the jury.

• *Be Responsible for All the Evidence*

In the minds of the jurors, there is one story, one case they are asked to judge. There is no such thing as plaintiff's evidence and defendant's evidence—there is just the evidence of the case. Most jurors, unaware of the nuances of discovery, believe that each attorney has access to all relevant evidence and simply picks and chooses what evidence to present and what evidence to leave out. The jury therefore holds each attorney responsible for the entirety of the evidence. This means that the jury expects you to present your good evidence but also to respond to the evidence that harms your case. If you fail to respond to harmful evidence or explain why it is irrelevant, jurors assume that you are unable to respond to or explain it. Therefore, the attorney must not only present evidence advantageous to his side but she must also address negative evidence. As one juror put it:

> *"You know, this guy has been working on this for six or seven years, and he had stacks and stacks of stuff. How he could have missed—and I don't remember exactly what this one thing was — but it was like how did he miss that? And it had to do with her medical records or something like that… And he could have still won—that wouldn't have made me decide any different, but, you know, in my mind I'm thinking he's not really got it all together."*

Jurors have three very realistic expectations during trial. First, jurors expect the attorneys from both sides of the case to have mastered all of the evidence. The jury frowns upon an attorney's failure to know all of the evidence, especially when litigation has spanned multiple years. The fact that the case is complex or that there are thousands of documents does not alleviate this expectation. Jurors know that the attorney is paid to know the case and have a superior understanding of the evidence. The attorney's method of trial presentation appears far more transparent when he knows the evidence inside and out.

The second expectation that the jury has is that the attorneys will cleanly lay out all the relevant information. This we break into two parts. First, you must be clear in your questions and explanation of the case. You are a paid advocate for your client—a fact the jury knows well. If you are unable to make your points cleanly and clearly, the jurors will not blame themselves and try harder to understand you. Instead, they will blame you for making things convoluted and difficult to understand. Worst of all, they will quit listening to your confusing narrative. Second, you must distill your case down to the essentials. And by essential we mean the facts necessary to prove your case and the facts necessary to explain or defend the damaging facts your opponent will be relying on. If you can be clear and focus on the essential, you will have gone a long way to insure a happy and attentive jury.

The jury wants the attorneys to present the facts of the case without leaving anything out. The jury does not appreciate feeling that facts have been hidden from them. Finally, the jurors anticipate that the attorneys will simply make arguments concerning the meaning of the evidence. To most effectively present our case to the jury, we must keep these expectations in mind when preparing for trial.

• *Jurors Hate Bench Conferences*

Seeking multiple bench conferences is one of the worst things you can do to your relationship with the jury. First, the jurors consider it a waste of their time. The lawyers have had years to get this case ready for trial, and they are supposed to know the law. If this is the case, jurors wonder why the attorneys keep running up to talk to the judge? Jurors believe the attorneys are being inconsiderate of their time. That is bad and annoying to jurors, but the real damage lies in the second problem.

When attorneys object and ask the judge to keep some evidence out, we hurt our credibility with the jury. The jury wants to make the right decision. And, what do we all need to make the best decision? We need all the facts, with nothing hidden from us. So when attorneys stand up in court and ask the judge to exclude certain evidence, are we helping or hurting the jury's decision-making ability? Clearly, there are legal reasons certain evidence is inadmissible, but that is not how the jury sees it. The jury sees you trying to keep facts and information from them.

Even when the judge says your objection is right, the jury is still going to wonder why you, the attorney, wanted to keep evidence from them. Listen to what the jurors said about how frustrating bench conferences are:

> *"The worst part [of serving on a jury] is you know there's more to the story, but for some reason or other you don't get to hear the whole story. Maybe there are things that aren't allowed in court that you're not allowed to hear, or maybe it was a deal that had been made between them that we won't talk about this, or maybe they're just not asking the right questions. But I think that is the single most frustrating thing is you do feel like you don't have the whole story."*

• *Tell the Whole Story*

It would undoubtedly prove frustrating to read a novel in which every other page was missing. Although the reader could glean a general notion of what had transpired in a partially intact book, he or she would be forced to bridge the gaps with guesses and assumptions in order to form a complete story. Jurors are asked to do something similar when lawyers and judges ask them to reach factual conclusions without giving jurors the full story. Jurors understandably grow irritated when asked to reach a decision knowing they have not been given the full story.

Telling the jury literally every single, relevant fact is impossible and a waste of time. First of all, no juror wants all of the facts. How does a slow, boring nine-day movie sound to you? Second, the parties have neither the time nor the resources to allow their advocates to fully address each piece of evidence. Finally, the rules of evidence often prevent us from disclosing certain information to the fact-finders. Despite the impracticality of apprising the jury of each and every detail of the case, the attorney can still leave the jury with the impression of transparency and that all essential facts have been entirely disclosed by doing two things: (1) arranging the facts in such a way that they logically tell a story and (2) avoiding glaring omissions.

During the trial, the effective advocate communicates to the jury a complete story. The attorney does this by taking all of the evidence and organizing it in a way that makes logical sense. Although the attorney may be able to convey a seemingly complete story with only the evidence beneficial to his case, the most effective trial attorney even responds to facts that are harmful to his side of the case when telling his story. Otherwise, the negative evidence will stick out like a sore thumb in the minds of the jurors. Your opponent will not hesitate to capitalize on your incomplete story. Failing to address the whole story and waiting for opposing counsel to complete the story has the potential to devastate an attorney's credibility. This is exactly what we heard from numerous jurors. Here is one particularly insightful juror's explanation of what happens when an attorney fails to address damaging facts.

"The plaintiff's attorney had facts that helped his case, but it was like he was leaving some stuff out that the other attorney would bring up. It's like what do they call it when you're lying by omission? I'm not lying to you, but I'm not telling you everything. He was giving us facts that were true, but they weren't the whole truth. And the other attorney always seemed to have the rest of the story, so the other attorney kind of lost a little bit of his credibility with me in that regard."

By addressing and explaining facts disadvantageous to our case, we can effectively preempt many of our opponent's arguments and demonstrate our own credibility to the jury. There are two primary ways to deal with damaging evidence. First, if you have the ammunition you can attack it and discredit it. This is often a hard thing to do because you must have iron-clad evidence that directly contradicts the negative evidence. Nibbling around the edges is not going to cut it. If you cannot disprove the fact, do not try this approach. Second, you can limit the effect of the bad evidence. By this, we mean show the jury why even in the face of the "bad" testimony or evidence, you still prevail. For example, repeated statements that the company had been experiencing financial difficulty and could not pay is an explanation but it is not a legally meritorious defense to a breach of contract case. This needs to be made clear to the jury.

• *Avoid Gaps*

Attorneys must be aware of how the jury will potentially construe trial proceedings and act accordingly. More specifically, lawyers must be conscious of how the jury interprets perceived gaps in the evidence. Juries do two things when faced with a gap in the evidence. First, they suspect that the parties or the attorneys are hiding something. And second, jurors fill the perceived gap with their own life experiences (which may or may not have anything to do with your case):

"There was just some gaps of evidence there in which maybe if those gaps—those invoices and receipts—could have been presented. Then we could have got a clearer picture of what really was purchased and what went on and what happened. And as a juror, we were just wondering, okay, someone is trying to hide something that they just don't want to come out."

Jurors notice when all of the evidence isn't presented to them. Of course, the rules of evidence typically prohibit the lawyer from disclosing to the jury all of evidence relevant to the case. Yet, the typical juror, unaware that hearsay and privilege prevent a lawyer from admitting certain evidence, interprets missing evidence to mean that the lawyers are concealing important facts.

"They were playing an audiotape that the sheriff's deputy had made with the defendant. As they were playing it, it was about to get to a part of the tape they didn't want us to hear yet and so they had to stop that and that was part of the evidence that of course left us in the jury room, okay, what else is on the tape? What else do we need to hear that we're not hearing? So that

---

> **was probably something that should have been done better
> from the prosecuting attorney.**"

Although the judge instructs the jury to consider only the evidence presented during trial, it is human nature to try to determine what has been left out. The attorney should be mindful of leaving the impression that something is missing. This is especially the case when the attorney has control over how to present the evidence. For instance, rather than obviously cutting deposition testimony short, the attorney could modify the tape (with opposing counsel's knowledge or the judge's permission, of course) so as not to present the jury with a glaring omission. By giving the jury the impression that they have received the complete story, the lawyer deters the jury from trying to fill in evidentiary gaps and ensures that the jury will appropriately focus solely on the evidence presented during trial when deliberating.

By leaving a blatant hole in the evidence, the attorney encourages the jury to assume facts. The jury's guessing at the missing evidence is much like a person playing a game of *Mad Libs*, a word game in which one player prompts another for a list of words to fill in blanks in a story. The player completing the blanks simply chooses words at random without having been apprised of the context of the anecdote. Because the player lacks a contextual basis, the words the player selects are often inappropriate and therefore quite humorous. An attorney's leaving gaps in the evidence, thereby forcing the jury to fill in the blanks themselves, ends up being similar to the word game. Unlike the players of *Mad Libs*, the jury is familiar with the context when completing the blanks; nevertheless, the jury's guesses at the evidence are often as inappropriate as a player's word choice in *Mad Libs*. What is amusing in *Mad Libs* is far less humorous in a trial. To avoid a potentially disastrous result, the attorney should fill in the gaps himself and enable the jury to intelligently decide the case.

• *No More Peek-a-Boo*

If you have played peek-a-boo with your children then I am sure you have witnessed the wonderful thought processes of a child.

When a two-year-old covers her eyes as part of the game, her world goes dark and she thinks she is safely hidden from the world in this darkness. As adults, we know that covering your eyes neither hides you nor makes it all go away. You can still be seen, you can still be found, and none of your problems go away. But why is it that so many lawyers act like two-year-olds and close their eyes believing that the bad facts will go away or no one will see them? Rather than shutting his eyes in an attempt to evade damaging facts, the attorney must face head-on all of the evidence including that which is detrimental to his side of the case.

In addition to addressing each fact of the case, the lawyer must also confront everything involved in the trial process, including circumstances beyond the actual trial. For instance, in a high profile case, the attorney should note who is paying attention to the case and why. Ideally, jurors wear blinders throughout the duration of the trial, but realistically they do not. Jurors are almost always exposed to the world outside the courtroom via the media and other individuals. In a high profile case, unless the judge cloisters the jury, inevitably the jury will become aware of widely-publicized "facts." Assuming the situation warrants it, the lawyer should incorporate well-known information surrounding the circumstances of the trial. Alternatively, the attorney should remind the jury that they are not to consider evidence they hear beyond the courtroom, although realistically the attorney cannot prevent the jurors from being at least subconsciously impacted by events taking place outside the trial proceedings. By failing to address the circumstances surrounding a high profile case, the lawyer misses the opportunity to influence the jury and leaves the jury to their own devices in determining how to address information they receive outside the courtroom.

Two-year-olds are cute but not effective advocates. An attorney has no hope of succeeding at trial if he covers his eyes and avoids evidence or other negative information regarding the case. Regardless of whether the lawyer addresses the facts or pretends that the facts do not exist, the jury will hear them if you face an opponent of any merit. Ignoring the facts will not prevent them from reaching the jury. By ignoring the facts, the attorney merely misses an opportunity to persuade the jury and surrenders a significant portion of his credibility.

• *Appropriately Deal with Objections*

Concerning objections, the average juror makes conclusions based on (1) whether the attorney asks the question or objects to the question, and (2) whether the judge sustains or overrules the objection. With respect to the asking attorney, the jury reaches the conclusion that the attorney is trying to be sneaky regardless of whether the judge sustains or overrules the objection. Regarding the objecting attorney, on the other hand, the judge's ruling determines how the jury views the attorney.

However the judge rules on the objection, the jury believes the asking attorney is trying to admit inappropriate evidence—otherwise, why would the other party object? The oft-objected-to lawyer comes across as trying to manipulate the system thereby undermining the attorney's credibility with the jury. With this in mind, the attorney should structure his witness examinations to avoid objections from opposing counsel. Limiting questions to matters that lie within the bounds of the evidentiary rules prevents opposing counsel from making legitimate objections; unfortunately, this will not prevent baseless objections.

How the jury views the objecting attorney depends on whether the judge sustains or overrules the objection. When the judge sustains an objection, the jury perceives that the objecting attorney has succeeded in concealing evidence. Because the jury assumes that the attorney objecting to the evidence is trying to hide something, the habitually objecting attorney appears non-transparent. By constantly making objections, the lawyer reminds the jury that he has an agenda and is not merely there to neutrally relay the facts, thereby inhibiting the attorney's ability to persuade the jury. Therefore, the lawyer should object as infrequently as possible. Does that mean never object? No, there are facts, like those dealing with insurance or settlement, that have no place in the record at any time and we must protect the record. But as far as general form objections, there is little to be gained by repeatedly making your adversary rephrase his question. And much of your own credibility can be lost in the process.

On the other hand, when the judge overrules an objection, the jury still believes the asking attorney is being conniving but reaches no conclusion with respect to the objecting attorney. The judge overruling an objection is the only situation in which the objecting attorney gets off scot-free from the jury's negative perceptions concerning objections.

By understanding how jurors typically perceive objections, the lawyer can often avoid causing the jury to negatively perceive him. The attorney does this by carefully structuring his witness examinations and by making selective objections.

Aside from taking into account how jurors view objections in general, the attorney must also be mindful of how jurors will perceive each individual objection.

"But they, you know, objected quite often, you know, saying they hadn't been shown materials and things like that. That seemed kind of odd since the case—or the actual accident occurred four years ago. And so it's like you would have thought you'd have seen everything by then."

Here is the interesting thing about this. When a juror hears an objection that something was not produced or had not been seen previously, they blame the objector for not doing his homework. From the lawyers' point of view, there are lots of explanations like it was not available or the other side hid it from him. But this is not what the jurors hear or see. They just see a lawyer standing up in court saying he has not seen it before. Because jurors know that the lawyer has been involved in the case for a while, they expect him to know everything and have seen everything about the case. When he stands up in court and says he has not seen something, the jury thinks he has failed to prepare properly. Objecting to not having seen something after several years of litigation justifiably raises the jurors' eyebrows.

• *Admit It When You Make a Mistake*

During trial, the attorney's primary goal is to give all the relevant evidence so the jury can reach factual conclusions. The lawyer simultaneously conveys evidence and makes arguments about what that evidence means. We need the jury to trust in our version of the case, so establishing and maintaining credibility is key. Unfortunately, making mistakes while relaying information is virtually unavoidable. How the attorney deals with his own mistakes and how he instructs witnesses to handle theirs plays a large part in whether the jury believes in his transparency.

Inevitably, due to the complexity of cases and the sheer volume of evidence that must sometimes be presented, mistakes will be made while the facts are being relayed. This is especially true for lawyers and for expert witnesses. An attorney may erroneously state facts because he has so many balls in the air. The attorney is always multi-tasking and the case at hand is never the only thing on his plate.

Concerning expert witnesses, lawyers usually call an expert to the stand because he or she is knowledgeable in a complex field. Frequently, the expert will not have dealt with all the facts of the case directly and will be asked bizarre hypothetical questions, so it is understandable that the expert may confuse a fact or two.

Fact witnesses can unintentionally misstate facts. A lay witness confuses facts because he becomes nervous on the witness stand. He is being asked to discuss a subject that is difficult for any number of potential reasons.

Fortunately, as fellow human beings, jurors understand that "to err is human." Although jurors empathize with attorneys and witnesses who inadvertently blunder during trial, jurors expect people to own up to their mistakes. The jury, like America at large, appreciates and forgives a person who takes responsibility for his behavior. The Bill Clinton/Monica Lewinsky debacle serves as a prime example of the value of admitting one's mistake. When President Clinton's inappropriate relationship with White House intern Monica Lewinsky became public, President Clinton initially denied that the two had "sexual relations." America did not believe Clinton. Eventually, Clinton held a prayer breakfast and took responsibility for his actions:

> *"It is important to me that everybody who has been hurt know that the sorrow I feel is genuine: First and most important, my family; also my friends, my staff, my Cabinet, Monica Lewinsky and her family, and the American people. I have asked all for their forgiveness."*

He fully and sincerely apologized to America. Although Clinton's sexual misadventures greatly disappointed the American public, his apology set the stage for forgiveness and ultimately allowed the country to move on.

Whatever the cause to which the attorney or witness attributes his error, it is important that he admit his mistake as soon as possible. Once an attorney or a witness gets caught in a error, acknowledging the error will not repair the lawyer's or witness's credibility with the jury. It proves far more difficult and therefore seems more genuine when a person owns up to a mistake prior to its discovery. When the person waits until after someone has noticed the error, the question of whether the person would have apologized had he not been caught will plague the jury's mind. We used the words error and mistake here because if you or your witness is ever caught in a lie, then there is little that can be done to rehabilitate credibility. You can apologize all you want, but if the jury believes that you or your client deliberately misled them, then you and your client deserve whatever the jury gives you as punishment.

Rule 7:
Get To The Point

The Declaration of Independence is the first lawsuit in American history. The document is an indictment of the ways of the British Empire, a list of grievances, and a declaration that the thirteen American colonies were an independent nation. The primary author of the Declaration of Independence, Thomas Jefferson, served as the first Secretary of State and third president of the United States. He is widely regarded by scholars to be one of the greatest American presidents because of his ability to effectively use the spoken and written word. Notwithstanding his fluency in five languages and his personal library of over 6,000 books, President Jefferson knew the importance of brevity: "The most valuable of all talents is that of never using two words when one will do." Our jurors resoundingly agree with this statement.

• *Less Is More*

Attorneys need to go into their cases with a clearly-defined and well-organized plan. They should know what they need to prove and how they will prove it. Each case essentially boils down to the questions asked on the jury charge. The attorney should therefore keep the jury charge in mind when deciding what evidence to build his case around. He should not spend time arguing a point that the jury simply does not get to decide.

"One particular thing that the attorney did there that was really starting to aggravate us jurors is—apparently this particular— where the crime took place was actually in the garage of this house. And he asked every witness how many doors were in that garage and some witnesses didn't remember there being a back door and some did. And so we probably went through twenty or thirty witnesses and [the attorney] just went through this long period of time of how many doors, how many doors, how many doors? And we kind of were joking with ourselves in the jury room—fine, we concede there were three doors. Just stop asking those same questions over and over again, because that was really getting annoying to us."

Prior to trying the case, you should distinguish between the important facts and the irrelevant ones. Don't try to prove a point simply because a fact is disputed. Jurors grow frustrated when the attorney spends an inordinate amount of time on something that is immaterial to the jury charge. Keep your eye on the prize—convincing the jury to believe your side of the case concerning the true disputes of the case—and avoid distracting yourself and the jurors with irrelevant albeit potentially interesting facts.

> *"And when I say less is more, it's like in a sense, just give the facts. But depending on what kind of lawyer you are, you're going to try to be more creative and I can understand that, but I have a problem with just hearing the same thing over and over. And maybe, you know, just going into too many details for somebody that you just picked off the street to come in and do jury duty. Maybe that may be too much for them, and it may confuse them."*

German architect Ludwig Mies van der Rohe is known for inventing the concept "less is more" and for buildings that embody this principle. Van der Rohe, a minimalist architect, believed that buildings should be designed with clarity and simplicity. Like other minimalists, he thought the best work was created by stripping it down to its most fundamental features. Like a vinter pruning his grapevines, Van der Rohe eliminated extraneous architectural features and kept only those structural details which served a functional purpose.

French aviator and writer Antoine de Saint-Exupéry expressed a similar philosophy in his memoir *Wind, Sand and Stars*. In the memoir, Exupéry recounts his experience when he and his navigator crashed in the Libya-Saharan desert in 1935. Stranded in the middle of a desert with little food and no water, the two Frenchmen began hallucinating after only a few days. While telling his story, Exupéry expressed his worldview and what he finds important in life. He notes that "perfection is achieved, not when there is nothing more to add, but when there is nothing left to take away." Attorneys would do well to adopt a "less is more" philosophy in trial. The more simply and concisely you present the facts and convey your arguments, the more readily the jury can process the information.

"The wrongful death case that I was in, I think that the mother's lawyer—the deceased mother's lawyer—could have been more convincing if he hadn't given so much detail. And the plaintiff was very honest and to the point and just 'let's cut to the chase' and 'these are the facts.'"

Streamline the case and only present what is absolutely necessary. By whittling down the case to its bare essentials, you focus the jury's attention on the true disputes of the case and avoid distracting them with irrelevant or tangential issues.

"[The defendant's attorney] had a way of speaking that was just—it's hard to explain, but he knew what he was going to say before he ever said it. And he was—he didn't drone on about things. He just got right to the point, asked his questions, and all of them seemed to matter. They were not just asking questions to kill time or whatever. It seemed like the other guy did that from time to time so he could thumb through some of his notes. [The defendant's attorney] was just way more concise in the way he spoke and the questions that he asked. He just seemed like he knew what he was doing."

Concisely presenting a case inspires confidence. The jury finds the attorney who quickly gets to the point far more competent than the overly verbose attorney.

• *Genuinely Be Prepared—You Can't Fake It*

The best way to focus your evidentiary presentation is to know exactly what you want to communicate before you walk into the courtroom for voir dire. Jurors can tell if you are organized and have your case planned out before you begin.

"A convincing attorney to me is one who has all his evidence well planned out and, well, makes a good presentation I would say with his evidence that he has prepared. The problem is I feel like the attorney may not have done his homework as well as he should have, and as a result he's reaching for straws and pulling straws. And as a result, he's not as convincing as he should be."

How credible the jury finds the attorney directly correlates with the depth of the attorney's preparation. In order to thoroughly prepare, the attorney must digest documents, interview witnesses, and read depositions. The attorney cannot fake tediously inspecting documents, meticulously interviewing witnesses, and otherwise diligently working on the trial.

"They were both very good. I thought that one was more prepared than the other. There was some evidence presented by the defendant that the plaintiff didn't know about. And in my opinion he should have because it could have prevented the whole trying from occurring."

Not only must the attorney acquire a superior understanding of the evidence, but he must also think through the evidence and its implications prior to the commencement of trial. Attorneys enjoy thinking aloud—this is undoubtedly beneficial during the preparation stages but is not acceptable at trial. The jury can discern whether the attorney formulates an idea for the first time during trial or whether the attorney preconceived his plan. Juries expect the attorney to have contemplated the evidence and created his arguments in advance of trial so that he flawlessly presents the evidence. The attorney should know in advance which questions to ask the witness and in what sequence to ask them.

> *"Well, I think the quality of the evidence is more important than the quantity. You know, one very important fact that you can prove is more important than the scattering of little bits and pieces."*

> *"The plaintiff's attorney—he provided a lot of information. He provided pictures of the area, but it just seemed like he was— he wasn't quite prepared for the case."*

A voluminous amount of evidence is no substitute for preparation and does not fool the jury. Jurors can tell when an attorney is simply trying to fill space. Everything the attorney does—every question that he asks and every document that he admits—should serve a purpose. If you can't come up with a reason to ask a particular question, the question is probably irrelevant and a space-filler. Filling space irritates the jurors because they believe their time is being wasting. Filling space accomplishes nothing; it is done without purpose.

> *"Well, one of the attorneys stood out in my mind because he didn't have like all the paperwork together. He just kept digging for paperwork. And I felt like, if you're an attorney, you should have all stuff together right there. When you go to court and trial and all this stuff, you should have all your information before you."*

The jury expects to see capable attorneys trying cases. When you fumble with exhibits and stammer when questioning witnesses, you appear incompetent and lose credibility. Flying by the seat of your pants, unsure of which exhibit to present at what time and which question to ask the next witness, does not come across well to the jury.

> *"I felt that the information could have been presented a little more efficiently and expediently. There are items that could*

> *have been rehearsed and/or set up before they were being*
> *presented—meaning the equipment should have been ready to*
> *go. It should have been cued—hit a button instead of fumbling*
> *around to try to get the computer to where it needed to be."*

Think of a trial as you would the production of a play. In a play, prior to the audience's arrival, the cast has rehearsed, the costumes have been created, and the props have been prepared. The audience expects a seamless production. They have no desire to see the backstage crew fumbling with the lights and the cast members searching for their props and costumes. Likewise, jurors expect the attorneys to be well-prepared. They want a smooth presentation of the evidence and do not wish to watch attorneys fumbling around. The jurors' role is to listen to the evidence and reach factual conclusions—don't waste their time by being ill-prepared. Simply taking the time to learn how to work the projector and cue a video deposition goes a long way with the jury.

• *Keep Your Presentation Flowing*

Attorneys should exude readiness. Repeatedly asking for breaks does not come across to the jury as the behavior of a well-prepared attorney, and you risk making the jurors feel their time is being wasted. Unless something beyond your control occurs (for example, opposing counsel knocks water on the attorney's side or someone becomes sick), continue with the case. Anything less than an hour is an unnecessary break and wastes everyone's time.

Taking breaks halts the process, extends the trial, and irritates the jurors. When the bailiff, court reporter, and jurors—none of whom have a vested interest in the case—are prepared to work longer and harder than the attorney, it reflects badly on the attorney and also the attorney's client. The frequently-breaking attorney appears both unprepared and disrespectful of the process.

If a break is absolutely necessary and within the attorney's control, he should ask for the break at a logical stopping point. Otherwise, the break interrupts the flow of the case. Movie-goers would not like a film being paused intermittently. Similarly, jurors dislike an attorney's taking a break in the middle of a witness's telling a story.

• *Vary Your Method of Presentation*

The attorney needs to leave a lasting impression on the jury. Dryly delivering the facts of the case will not do the trick. The attorney effectively communicates to the jury by utilizing multiple sensory channels, creatively presenting the evidence, and repeating important facts and central arguments.

Teachers often use multi-sensory methods of teaching to enhance their students' ability to retain information. Attorneys should use similar principles in the courtroom to ensure that the jurors can repeat the important facts and arguments during deliberations. An instructor using multi-sensory methods teaches her students by simultaneously appealing to a variety of the students' senses. By hitting the students' visual, auditory, and tactile senses, the teacher multiplies the students' opportunities to retain knowledge.

Use a multi-sensory method of teaching in the courtroom to aid the jury in remembering the facts and retain your arguments. By simultaneously utilizing different sensory channels, you enhance the jurors' ability to retain information. For example, concerning one fact, the attorney might question a witness, provide a demonstration, and present a chart thereby engaging the jurors' auditory and visual senses by having the jurors listen to and observe a witness, watch a demonstration, and examine a chart. By conveying the same information in a variety of ways, you keep the jury engaged throughout the trial and leave a lasting impression. This is how to keep the jurors focused on the goal.

To further enhance communication, the attorney also needs to tailor the way that he presents each case. A cookie-cutter presentation often fails to fit the mold of the particular trial at hand and therefore proves ineffective. In his book *Beyond Bullet Points*, Cliff Atkinson discusses how to craft and deliver a successful

PowerPoint presentation. Atkinson criticizes the basic, untailored, bullet-point-based PowerPoint template as uninteresting and unhelpful. According to Atkinson, to effectively deliver a PowerPoint presentation, the speaker should do more than merely read bullet points from a slide. The speaker should be creative in his delivery and help jurors focus on key points. For instance, the presenter could pass something around for the audience to physically hold while watching the PowerPoint presentation. Doing something as simple as engaging the audience members' tactile sense makes the presentation more interesting; and the more interested the audience, the more likely they are to retain the point you are trying to make.

While representing the plaintiff in Ernst v. Merck in 2005, the first of several highly publicized lawsuits surrounding the drug Vioxx, trial attorney Mark Lanier championed the principles discussed in *Beyond Bullet Points*. Seeking an unconventional method with which to present his case, Lanier consulted Atkinson. Most notable is the two and a half hour opening statement that Lanier delivered without notes. Lanier used clear, simple language, readily understandable to the jurors. In the typical opening statement, the attorney verbally tells the jury a story. Lanier did something different; he accompanied his story with PowerPoint slides and overhead projections. By incorporating PowerPoint slides into his opening statement, Lanier thoroughly engaged the jury and helped them to visualize his case. *Fortune* [August, 2008] called his method of presentation "frighteningly powerful." The fact that the jury returned a verdict in favor of Lanier's client suggests that his method is effective.

When preparing for trial, consider how Lanier approached the Ernst v. Merck case. By creatively conveying the evidence and by tailoring the method of presentation to each particular trial, you can ensure that you get your point across to the jury.

Multi-sensory methods and creative presentations undoubtedly prove helpful; yet, the best and surest way to leave a lasting impression with the jury is via repetition. According to German psychologist Hermann Ebbinghaus, repetition proves crucial to memory retention.

After researching and experimenting with memory, Ebbinghaus discovered that how much information a person remembers or forgets directly correlates with (1) the passage of time and (2) the number of times the information was repeated. He found that after a mere two days, a person retains less than thirty percent of what he learned. However, repeating the information conditions the mind and enables a person to remember a far greater percentage than he would otherwise. Teachers and professors utilize Ebbinghaus' philosophy on memory daily when they repeat material to help their students get the point.

Attorneys recognize the importance of the jury's retaining the important case facts as well as attorney arguments. If the jury forgets or distorts facts relevant to the central issues of the case, the jury cannot possibly reach its best decision. The attorney needs to present the evidence to the jury clearly and memorably. To ensure that the jurors remember the evidence presented during trial, the attorney must repeat the important facts and central arguments to the jurors.

• *Challenges and Opportunities with Deposition Testimony*

> *"Most of the testimony was via deposition. And it was read to us, which was a little troublesome because when you have the individual in front of you, there's body language that goes along with everything that is said. And sometimes the body language speaks louder than words."*

Jurors want to see witnesses in the flesh and blood. They want to watch the witness as the attorney questions him and observe the witness' body language and demeanor when he responds. Jurors greatly prefer live witnesses over video deposition witnesses and frequently complain about attorneys subjecting them to video and written depositions.

The attorney should endeavor to present only live witnesses to the jury. However, if a video deposition absolutely cannot be avoided, make the deposition as bearable as possible for the jury by cutting it down, providing an introduction, and setting the jurors' expectations concerning the video.

> *"And there were a lot of things that I didn't need to see. I didn't need to see three minutes of that doctor flipping pages trying to figure out what he was looking at. Because really that served to negate the validity of his testimony."*

You can avoid wasting the jurors' time by presenting only what is essential. If you must use a video deposition, break the video into short segments, to its bare essentials. The jurors' attention span for watching video depositions, as opposed to hearing from live witnesses, is much shorter, and jurors loathe being subjected to hours and hours of video deposition. Plus, jurors lack the attention span to watch hours of video deposition. The average person's attention span is that of a thirty-minute sitcom (which is actually only twenty minutes if commercial breaks are taken into consideration). So keep the jurors' attention spans in mind when preparing the video deposition.

Be sure to ask the judge and opposing counsel if you can make a one or two minute introduction. It might consist of something like, "You are about to hear from Witness X who will tell you three important things." Or you could say, "You are about to watch a twenty-minute videotape, and I want you to look for three things." The jury appreciates an attorney's apprising them of the length of the video and telling them what to expect. Road mapping focuses the jury's attention and tells them what they should get out of the video.

A short introduction prior to starting the video deposition is extraordinarily helpful. Newscasters tease their viewers with impending news stories, making viewers want to come back for more. And movie producers show previews of their films prior to releasing them in order to attract an audience. Similarly, you should give the jury a brief synopsis of what will be discussed during the deposition. Make the introductory summary as fascinating as possible to pique the jury's interest.

Jurors find listening to attorneys read a deposition even more dreadful than watching a video deposition. With video depositions, the jury at least gets to hear the witness's tone and watch their mannerisms. With written depositions, the jurors get neither. They simply have to listen to the attorney read from a document. Having one attorney sit in the witness chair acting as the witness and reading the witness's responses while another attorney questions the witness minimizes but does not eliminate the agony caused by listening to a dry, monotonous written deposition.

• *Creatively Repeat Important Themes and Facts*

Although repetition undoubtedly proves crucial to the jurors' ability to remember the facts and arguments presented during trial, the most pervasive complaint jurors make is that the attorney sounded like a broken record. Jurors feel that attorneys grossly underestimate the jurors' intelligence and unnecessarily waste their time by repeating themselves.

The attorney faces competing interests during trial. On one hand, you need to condition the jury to remember the facts of the case. The surest way to guarantee that the jury does not forget important facts of the case is via repetition. On the other hand, a repetitious attorney irritates the jurors and causes them to tune out. Jurors do not appreciate being spoken to as though they are first-graders and view the attorney who repeats the exact same facts in the exact same ways as condescending.

"What stands out to me is the amount of time that seemed to be redundant. There were some times there it just seemed like we spent seeing the same things over and over and over. And it almost made you wonder, 'Do you not think we heard you the first time, the second time, the third time?' By the fourth time, it was like, 'Okay, we get it.'"

The jury undoubtedly notices when you repeat yourself. You do yourself no favors by pretending otherwise. Acknowledge to the jury that you understand you are repeating yourself but that there is a reason for the redundancy. By letting the jury know that you realize you are being redundant, you avoid making jurors feel that you are talking down to them. And by telling the jury that the reiteration serves a purpose, you prevent the jury from tuning you out after hearing a fact once.

For example, after eliciting a particular fact from one witness, you might want to draw out the same fact from a second witness. Acknowledge to the second witness, for the benefit of the jury, that you know the jury has already heard about the event from the first witness but that you want to hear what the second witness has to say about the occurrence to make sure that everyone is on the same page. By giving the jurors a reason for the redundancy, you prevent the jurors from feeling that you are wasting their time with needless repetition.

Another subtle method of getting information to jurors repetitively is to use roadmaps and signposts. By conveying important facts and arguments in different ways, you prevent the trial from becoming unbearably monotonous and unnecessarily lengthy. You get to the point.

But use redundancy sparingly and only repeat yourself when you have a clearly-defined purpose in mind. Reiterate only important facts and central arguments. Even if disputed, don't repeat peripheral facts because doing so ultimately serves no purpose.

"I didn't quite like the way the homeowner's attorney sometimes would ask a question. He'd get an answer, but then, too, he'd go right back and rephrase the question and rephrase the question again to get the same answer. The question had been answered, but he constantly reiterated and wanted the defendant to answer the same question over and over."

Never beat a dead horse.

Rule 8:
Stay Focused

The trial lawyer's singular goal is to effectively communicate the facts, themes, and conclusions in a clear and memorable way. Anything that distracts from this goal hurts his client's case. Elbert Hubbard, the accomplished American editor and writer, tells us the importance of having—and keeping—the attention of our audience: "All noise is waste. So cultivate quietness in your speech, in your thoughts, in your emotions. Speak habitually low. Wait for attention and then your low words will be charged with dynamite." Our goal as lawyers is to have our trial presentation charged with dynamite. Unfortunately, our jurors told us that lawyers often miss this mark.

In this chapter jurors describe how nervous ticks and mannerisms distracted them during trial, and we analyze the physiological and psychological affects on jurors when they are distracted. Jurors describe how they had competitions to decide how long an attorney would drag out the "o" in "so" before each question on cross-examination; or in another trial, they counted how many times an attorney twisted his eyebrow each day. One juror lamented the use of "air quotes" which, in his opinion, showed bad manners and caused jurors to fantasize about "coming out of the jury box if we could to tie his hands to his sides!" These stories are humorous unless you are the lawyer with the distracting habit. Ask yourself this question: if the jury is using its attention to count how many times you twist your eyebrows or if they are plotting to tie your hands to your side, what is the likelihood that the jurors are paying attention to the substance of your client's case?

• *Maintaining the Jury's Attention in a Twitter World*

Observing a trial is quite different from reading a book or watching a movie. If a person spaces off in the middle of reading a book, he can simply flip back a few pages and reread what he has missed. Likewise, if a person stops paying attention while watching a movie, catching up on the plot is merely a push of the rewind button away. Ongoing trials, on the other hand, have no rewind mechanism. When the jurors' minds wander, they miss vital testimony, crucial documents, and other important evidence.

Jurors are prohibited from discussing the case until deliberations. Once the time to deliberate arrives and the jurors may finally discuss the case amongst themselves, what the momentarily inattentive juror missed during the trial is already gone—it simply becomes an absent page in the story or a blank spot on the tape. Unless the attorney risks undue repetition, there is no way for a juror to get back what he missed. Therefore, it is essential that the attorney do everything possible to keep every juror's attention throughout the trial.

The best way to keep jurors engaged is by giving them a good show. The first step is good eye contact with the jury. As we discussed earlier, the jury denies their attention to the lawyer who keeps his head down and reads from a script. You cannot connect well to or communicate meaningfully with jurors when you bury your head in your notes. Not only do jurors find such a lackluster delivery horribly dull, they also find it distracting. We must avoid doing anything to draw the jury's attention away from the case.

• *Jurors Focus on the Negative*

When it comes to politicians, the public at large focuses more on the negative than on the positive. Campaigning politicians, understanding that negative events are more likely to pique the public's interest and are therefore more newsworthy than positive occurrences, participate in mudslinging. Rather than focusing on the merits of his opponent's platform, the campaigning politician delves into his opponent's past to uncover and reveal unsavory facts about his opponent. Unfortunately, the public has a one-track mind when it comes to the negative and has a difficult time putting the negative out of its mind. The career of a politician, even one who has acted nobly and is generally a good person, can be ended by the revelation of a single negative fact. Take Newt Gingrich for example. Gingrich was very popular within the Republican Party—he represented a congressional district in Georgia for several years, served as a U.S. congressman, and eventually became Speaker of the House. Democrats challenged the prominent

Republican by focusing on Gingrich's personal life. Rather than focusing on the political decisions Gingrich had made, many of which were considered positive, the media ran stories about his divorces and his affairs. Even the Republican Party which had so strongly backed Gingrich eventually deserted him, and finally the former Speaker resigned from his Speakership as well as from his congressional seat.

The negative simply leaves a stronger and a more lasting impression on people than the positive. Just as muscle in the body weighs more than fat, the negative outweighs the positive. Building a good reputation literally takes years; however, it takes mere seconds to destroy one. How jurors view attorneys is quite similar to how the public views politicians—jurors may take minor note of our positive traits but truly linger on our negative characteristics. We must avoid giving the jurors a reason to have a negative opinion of us. Viewing the attorney in a negative light automatically causes the jury to have a negative opinion of the attorney's case and client. When the jury begins to think of the attorney in negative terms, they stop paying attention to the evidence and focus instead on the attorney's demeanor. One juror found himself distracted by an attorney's cockiness.

"I found [the attorney] at times to seem kind of a little bit cocky, a little bit—some of the remarks he made just seemed kind of a little arrogant. I can't remember what they were, but I remember thinking at the time they seemed a little inappropriate."

No one likes to be around arrogant and cocky people. The reason is simple. We all know that arrogant and cocky people are consumed with themselves and proving they are better than everyone else. If jurors think you are arrogant or cocky or trying to prove you are better than they are, then they certainly will not be willing to be persuaded by the things that such attorneys say and do. If you are so labeled, your client and your case are in trouble.

• *Identify—and Avoid—Your Bothersome Mannerisms*

Jurors, like all of us, can be distracted. Often the evidence they hear is mundane and uninteresting, motivating them to look for other things with which to occupy their minds. The natural, human inclination for entertainment coupled with the judge's instructions to refrain from discussing the case until deliberations causes jurors to look to the people involved in trial for amusement. Because the lawyers essentially direct the show, the jury has an abundance of opportunities to observe and pass judgment on the lawyers. We need to realize that the jury constantly watches and critiques us. When we pick our noses, twirl our hair, or slurp our drinks, the jury is keenly aware. The jurors notice and gossip when a female attorney wears gaudy jewelry or a garish engagement ring or when she sits in an unladylike fashion.

The jurors sometimes find the attorney's mannerisms distracting. Once the jurors notice the irritating mannerisms, they find it difficult to focus on anything else. One juror revealed to us that an attorney who pulled at his eyebrows throughout the trial diverted the jury's attention. The same juror told us that another attorney, with undue frequency, said, "We know, you know" while presenting his case. During deliberations, the jury, rather than focusing on the evidence presented at trial, spent a great deal of time mocking the attorney.

"This is probably—all my fellow jurors would want me to say is that some of the attorneys had habits... We weren't like talking about the case but just talking about—for example, I think one of them had this habit of pulling his eyebrows. And so it constantly—it became distracting. Or one attorney would say 'We know, you know,' the way he would say it. So in the deliberating, we would go, 'We know.'"

Another juror told us that an attorney's twitchy mannerisms distracted the jury.

> *"On the plaintiff's side, the lawyer had a lot of distracting mannerisms—very twitchy. He seemed to flutter around a lot on his papers—things like that."*

Understandably, many of our habits are innate, and we are completely unaware of them. We must therefore make a conscious effort to avoid distracting the jury. When the jury's focus shifts from the evidence or testimony to the attorney and his demeanor, the jury is no longer paying attention to the case. We need to remember that the trial is about our client and the evidence, not us. One juror told us that an attorney's stealing the spotlight during trial sidetracked the jurors.

> *"But the lawyer that was representing the radio station or former station owners—I thought he was just way overboard. He was too aggressive. He was—I hope it was on tape, because I actually think he felt like he was making a movie. Because I remember even in the jury in the back we talked about—that guy, it's like somebody—because the judge kept saying 'cut.' And [the attorney] would just keep coming back."*

We should think of ourselves not as the main protagonists of the story but as behind-the-scenes directors or producers. We need to do our best to fade into the background, avoid doing anything that draws attention to ourselves, and let the evidence of our case take precedence.

• *Keep People on Your Side of the Case Under Control*

We need to keep our clients in check during trial. As much as the jurors are watching and evaluating the attorneys' behavior during the trial, they are judging our clients even more. Our clients are the ones whose lives we ask the jurors to change via their decisions. Jurors are very curious about our clients and therefore constantly watch them. The jury judges our client's demeanor as well as how our clients react to the evidence and to the testimony. We should remind our clients that the jurors are carefully scrutinizing them at all times during the trial. The jurors should strive to get to the heart of the case and to learn of our client's true self. Jurors believe, and perhaps accurately so, that a person acts more genuinely when he is not being publicly questioned and is less aware that he is being watched. Therefore, our clients need to act appropriately throughout the duration of the trial, especially when they are not on the witness stand. One way to remember this is to use what we call the one minute rule. Tell your client that once he gets within a mile of the courtroom, they need to assume they are being watched by the jurors.

We must also keep in check those who are in the courtroom on behalf of our client. The jury is familiar with and will apply the maxim "you are the company you keep." The demeanor and actions of those present on behalf of our clients directly reflects on our clients. We must keep in mind that any friends or family of the client who attend the trial provide additional opportunities to distract the jury. One juror told us that the plaintiff's family diverted the jury—one adult family member constantly readjusted his crutch while the plaintiff's child frolicked about the courtroom.

"I don't know if it was deliberate or inadvertent, but the plaintiff's family moved constantly. One had a disability and a crutch and so he was constantly readjusting himself and the crutch would hit things and things like that. They also brought a child with them and so she would play and do different things and move about the court, and there was entry in and out of the court. So you'd be distracted a little bit and you'd have to bring yourself back."

Jurors should not have to force themselves to tear themselves away from interesting diversions and pay attention to the trial. A less than conscientious juror will not make a conscious effort to focus on the evidence we present. We need to facilitate the jurors hearing and understanding the evidence as opposed to diverting the jurors' attention with unnecessary distractions.

• *Sate the Jurors' Curiosity*

We only present the jury with facts that are directly pertinent to the case at hand and are admissible under the rules of evidence. However, we must be mindful that certain references we make during trial pique the jurors' interest, distracting them. We need to consider what the jury will want to know and then satisfy their curiosity as early in the trial as possible. One juror informed us that the entire jury was just dying to meet a woman who had dated both the plaintiff and the defendant.

"In the last case, we had this lady who—she was a blonde bombshell, and she had dated both sides of the fence, you know, the franchisee and the franchisor, and she had dated both of them. And it was just—everyone was just dying to meet her, you know. We kept thinking, when is she coming in? What is she going to look like?"

We need to consider what seemingly unimportant details the jury will focus on and address them. By telling the jurors what they want to know, we avoid disappointing and distracting them by sating their curiosity.

• *Focus on the Merits*

The trial attorney should not argue simply for argument's sake but should focus on the true disputes of the case. By concentrating on the real issues, the attorney streamlines the case and turns the jury's attention to what they will be deciding after the attorneys have presented the evidence. When you fail to focus on the real disputes of the case, you essentially bog down the jurors' minds with unnecessary information which makes it difficult for the jury to decide the case on an appropriate basis.

"[The prosecutor] was very effective getting his point across. No B. S.—just here's the evidence. I'm just going to throw it at you and it's up to you to take into consideration to help with your deliberations to, you know, make a good decision."

One way to focus the jury on the key issues is by being straightforward—candidly tell the jury what you and your client do not dispute. For example, if all the parties agree that a valid contract existed, then disclose that to the jury. This is far more effective than an attorney who pretends that there is a litany of disputed facts when there is really only one major issue. Present the jury with the ball on a silver platter—don't hide the ball from them.

"I thought the defense attorney—the lady—did a very nice job. She really just stuck to the facts. She didn't present a lot of kind of extraneous information. I mean she really just kept it simple and stuck to the facts."

You can also point the jury in the right direction by specifically telling them in voir dire or opening statement: "The key disputes are A, B, and C, and the evidence will show X, Y, and Z." Disputes A, B, and C and Evidence X, Y, and Z become your outline for how to present the case. Be sure to address each major dispute and all the evidence relevant to the major disputes in the trial as the jury will certainly notice if you should fail to do so.

Another helpful way you can begin the case is by telling the jury in opening statement that you will prove three things. The three things that you will prove should each relate to the factual issues the jury will decide. For example, in a contract case, the attorney might tell the jury he will prove (1) that the parties had a contract, (2) that the opposing party did not fulfill the contact, and (3) that the client suffered X amount in damages. The first relates to duty, the second to breach, and the third to liability—each is something about which the jury will reach conclusions at the end of the trial. By telling the jury he will prove three disputed things, the attorney immediately implicates the merits and tells a short, comprehensive story of what he plans to prove.

Realistically consider the merits of the case when you decide to which issues to direct the jury's attention. After spending a good deal of time on the case, you should know precisely what you can and cannot prove. Concerning each central issue, the attorney should appreciate whether he has a slam dunk.

Rule 9:
Use PowerPoint Slides and Demonstratives Effectively

PowerPoint presentations are a wonderful multimedia communication tool, but they are too often abused rather than used to their full effect. "How can that be" you ask, "when everyone agrees that a picture is worth a thousand words?" Because more often than not, we use Power-Point slides not to project images; we use them to project text. We put up slides that look more like documents than images. Here's an example.

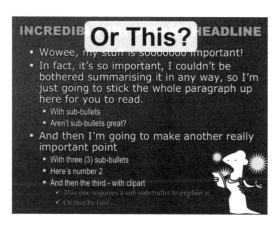

The power of a multimedia trial presentation lies not in the PowerPoint slides, but in the evidence—substantive and testimonial—as well as in the trial lawyer himself. The intent of the multimedia tool is to make the evidence, themes, and conclusions of the case more accessible and memorable.

People are tired of PowerPoint presentations because most PowerPoint slides simply present too much information for the human mind to handle. Typical slides filled with busy backgrounds, endless bullet points, and tangled diagrams cause the brain to shut down. This brain shutdown or "PowerPoint overload" kills persuasive communication and renders information inaccessible and forgettable. Bad multimedia presentations confuse and persuade no one.

A growing body of research explains the science behind Power-Point overload, and teaches that we need to shift our thinking; we can no longer expect audiences or juries to struggle to adapt to our inept use of PowerPoint slides. Instead, we must align our use of PowerPoint presentations to the way people learn.

• *Some Background*

It is amazing that PowerPoint presentations have been so widely adopted in thir relatively brief, seventeen-year life; but it is even more surprising that there is little research that informs their use. This research vacuum has been filled by conventional wisdom—commonly accepted beliefs that guide behavior. A good example is the "6 x 6 Rule"—no more than six lines of text on a PowerPoint slide, six words per line. Recent studies, however, establish that following the 6 x 6 Rule is a surefire way to cause PowerPoint overload. The same holds true for a number of other PowerPoint conventions, including using titles and shrinking text and visuals to make them fit on a slide.

The price of PowerPoint overload is ineffective communication. PowerPoint-based miscommunication is toxic. If the jury does not understand your PowerPoint presentation opening or is bored by your PowerPoint presentation closing, you have lost precious persuasion time. Forever.

Since the 1990s, Richard Mayer at the University of California, Santa Barbara, has conducted research studies on multimedia learning—how to combine words and pictures to promote understanding and retention. The studies have resulted in clear recommendations for multimedia design principles. This research marks a turning point for PowerPoint slides because it teaches us how to use this important tool based on the way the human mind works.

Most PowerPoint presentations look alike because PowerPoint software has certain features that make particular tasks easy. For example, PowerPoint slides are built around templates, so we use templates. PowerPoint software makes it easy to use bulleted lists, so we use bulleted lists. PowerPoint software makes it easy to paste many items on a slide, so we paste many items onto the slide.

Unfortunately, many PowerPoint templates and features contradict current research in cognitive science. Scientists know how the mind works. Richard Mayer, Professor of Psychology at the University of California, Santa Barbara, explains an overview of human cognitive processing in the book *Multimedia Learning*. Its core elements break down into three concepts: dual channel, limited capacity, and active processing.

Human beings have separate information processing channels for visual material and verbal material. The visual channel handles information presented to the eyes (such as illustrations, animation, video, or on-screen text). The verbal channel handles information presented to the ears (such as narration or nonverbal sounds). The constraints on our processing capacity force us to make decisions about which pieces of incoming information to pay attention to and the degree to which we should build connections between selected pieces of information and our existing knowledge.

We see this in our everyday lives all the time. Ladies, have you ever tried to get your husband to focus during the last quarter or inning of the telecast of his favorite team's game? Gentlemen, how about getting a response from your son in the middle of an X-Box battle? The mind can only take in so much information at one time.

As a presenter, you must be mindful of this and create a PowerPoint presentation that takes advantage of the dual-channel structure of the human information processing system by presenting complementary material in words and pictures.

Clearly, human beings have the ability to use both channels simultaneously, but they can pay attention to only a few pieces of information in each channel at a time. When an illustration or animation is presented, we are able to hold in our brains only a few of the images in working memory at one time. These images reflect portions of the presented material rather than an exact copy of the presented material. When a narration is presented, the listener can only hold a few words in working memory at any one time. "A jury," as Vincent Bugliosi once said, "remembers the tune but not the words."

In a PowerPoint context, the presenter must take into consideration the limited capacity of the information processing channels and minimize the chances of overloading the cognitive system.

Human beings understand presentations when they pay attention to the relevant material, organize it into a coherent mental structure, and integrate it with their prior knowledge. Humans are active processors who seek to make sense of multimedia presentations. With PowerPoint presentations, the presenter must promote active cognitive processing by guiding the processes of selecting, organizing, and integrating information. This means that you cannot just throw a bunch of data up on the screen. Instead you have to select, organize and present information in a means that is simple and accessible to your audience.

Our understanding of the way the mind works has three implications for PowerPoint presentations:

1) PowerPoint presentations should use both visual and verbal forms of presentation.

2) Filling the slides with information will quickly overload people's cognitive systems.

3) The presentations should help the audience to select, organize, and integrate presented information.

In the next few pages, we will look at how the juror interviews we conducted bear out each of these principles and will present suggestions for how to avoid problems with your multimedia message.

• *Ensure That Demonstratives Are Visible*

The purpose of using demonstratives is to help the jury put all of the pieces of the trial together and understand the case as a whole. Demonstratives should facilitate the trial process not make it more difficult. Carefully select the size and font for demonstratives. In this context, size does matter. The size of the font needs to be large enough so that the jurors can easily read the PowerPoint slide or demonstrative from across the courtroom in the jury box. The type of font is also an important consideration. Certain fonts are simply easier to read than others. San-serif fonts are generally the best for PowerPoint presentations and be sure to use a consistent font throughout the presentation and never use a font smaller than thirty points. Although cutesy fonts may delight us attorneys, unusual fonts prove difficult to read and therefore irritating to jurors.

Not only does the attorney need to be conscious of how he formats the demonstrative, but he also needs to ensure that the courtroom environment facilitates the jury's readily being able to see the demonstrative. One juror told us that poor lighting made it incredibly difficult to read items the attorneys placed on the projector.

"Well, this last case—this has absolutely nothing to do with the judge, but the room was very light. And when papers were put on the overhead projector—particularly handwritten papers—they were very difficult to see."

If the jury can't see it, the slide is worthless. And remember—some people have poor vision, and nearly everyone's vision deteriorates with age.

• *The Use of Multimedia Must Be Accessible*

If the jury doesn't understand, they will not remember it. Too many times, we have seen well-intentioned attorneys conceive of a great demonstration or a diagram to support their points, but they fumble and falter in the execution. The classic example is an intersection collision. I have watched students over the years struggle with presenting this issue. The case involves a pedestrian who was hit at a four-way intersection with a dedicated turn lane. Testimony about this kind of issue is always difficult. The car was heading north but turning west. The pedestrian was going east. Another car approached from the south. You have to be pretty good with spatial perception to follow this explanation. Then we complicate that because you will have two drivers, a pedestrian and three witnesses all testifying about what they saw from their unique vantage point. One says the northbound car was actually turning west. Another thought the pedestrian angled slightly to the south. If you are not totally lost by now, I guarantee that there is no way you can remember who said what about who was going where when. The easy way to handle that is with a chart or diagram, right? Not so fast. Is it going to be a on a poster board or a flat model? Are you going to draw movement like a cartoon or have movable cars for demonstrations? How are you going to distinguish what each witness said about what they saw? The answer depends on your individual case, but let's take a look at what one juror tells us about exactly this scenario.

"The only thing was that they could make some of their evidence a little easier to understand. And by that I mean there was a map—a diagram—that they were asking for as I said. A truck was involved and they were asking where the placement of the truck was and so on, and that got a little confusing. [T]hey talked about what was north, south, east, and west, but not people would go — 'I guess north, I guess a little more east, I guess maybe move the pen a little more west.' I think it would have helped just [to label] N, S, E, and W, so people could look at that as a reference point."

If you got confused during this quote, just think how confused the jurors got actually listening to this during trial. Our goal is to use visuals to make events accessible to the jurors and easy to understand.

• *Avoid Complex Slides*

Complex, cluttered slides prove problematic for two reasons. First, the jury spends too much time trying to dissect the slides and ultimately stops listening to the attorney. Second, the jurors grow weary of trying to understand what the complicated slides mean and stops putting forth effort to discern what the attorney is trying to convey. Simple slides, on the other hand, enable the jurors to look up, quickly read and digest the material, and return their attention to the attorney or witness speaking.

The jurors' main focus should be on the attorney or the witness not the image on the screen of his PowerPoint presentation. A person's visual sense trumps all other senses; so when the attorney gives the jury a demonstrative to look at, it will consume the jury's attention entirely. When attorneys show the jurors cluttered slides, they will spend time studying and reading those slides. The jurors lock in on their visual channels and their auditory channels shut down. At that point, although the jurors still hear the words of the attorney or witness, the jurors are no longer truly listening to what the attorney is saying. When we create each PowerPoint slide, we should keep in mind our purpose: to enhance, support, and emphasize what we are saying. We cannot accomplish this goal by using complex slides. Humans have a limited capacity for digesting and retaining information. Long, bulleted lists and overly saturated slides cause the jurors' minds to overload. When the jurors' minds overload, the jurors stop taking in and processing information. The attorney's slides may as well be in Greek or Japanese—they will prove completely foreign and utterly meaningless to the jurors. Our jurors have no vested interest in our cases and are therefore unwilling to work extremely hard simply to understand the message you are trying to convey.

So, attorneys should construct simple slides, conveying a single point, and enabling the jurors to pay attention to the oral presentation. The ideal slide has six words or less and/or an eye-catching image. Simple slides allow jurors to both engage their visual receptors and concentrate on what the attorney says. Here is a slide we used in closing to emphasize a piece of testimony by a witness.

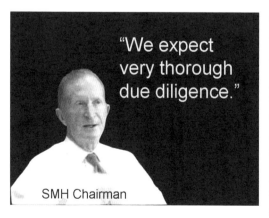

The point of this slide was to capture an image of the witness—in this case the Chairman of the company—and remind the jury exactly what he said. A juror can read and process this slide in about three seconds. Once they have read and processed the slide, their attention can return to the attorney presenting the closing where he can expound on this point or explain why this is such an important fact for their deliberations.

Use real images. No clip art. Although many attorneys find clip art cute and clever, most jurors deem it unprofessional and silly.

Rather than using clip art in your PowerPoint slides, use real images to convey your message with authority. For example, the attorney could include photographs of events leading up to the case in his PowerPoint slides. Pictures of real life events captivate the jury. One of my trials involved three brothers. Obviously, they all had the same last name so it would be confusing to call them by their last name. I wanted to prepare jurors for this potentially confusing issue early in the case, so I created a slide with all three brothers' pictures and their first names. Here it is:

Essentially, I used the slide to introduce the jurors to the main players in the action. Did this win the case? No, but I think it made the facts of the case more accessible because the jurors met the brothers pictorially at the very beginning.

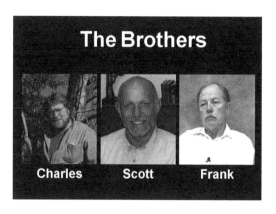

If you do not believe us about the value of pictures over clip art, listen to what the jurors had to say about the impact of pictures. One juror told us how effectively the attorney used pictures related to the case.

"The photographic evidence impacted me a great deal, and it just made me see clearly, I guess, what it was all about. It was traumatic—it was really traumatic."

If you want your message to have impact and meaning, use real pictures of real places and real people.

• *Provide a Roadmap*

As we discussed in *Rule 4: Set Expectations*, providing the jury with a roadmap of our case is essential. Present your roadmap during opening statement, giving the jury a brief overview of the case. The opening is so important because you are setting the stage. You want to give the jury a framework on which they can attach the evidence. In most trials, I start off by promising the jury that I will prove three things. I tell them that if I prove these three things they will have no choice but to reach a verdict in our favor. For example, here is a slide I used in the opening of a recent trial on behalf of two executives who claim they were wrongfully fired and therefore owed back pay and bonuses.

We Will Prove

1. **Exhibitions Division Had A Record Year.**

2. **Contract Mandated Bonus And Salary Increase.**

3. **Company's Breaches Are "Good Reason" To Terminates.**

My clients led the most successful division of the company to a record year. Instead of bonuses, they were terminated for no good reason. This was the basic story and the framework through which I wanted the jury to evaluate the evidence. This violates my six-word rule from earlier, but it does encapsulate the entire case in a single slide and explains why we should win.

I showed the jury this roadmap throughout the trial to keep them oriented and fresh on what the case was about and the proof they needed to be looking for.

Assuming the attorney proves what he told the jury he would prove

We Have Proved

1. **Exhibitions Division Had A Record Year.**

2. **Contract Mandated Bonus And Salary Increase.**

3. **Company's Breaches Are "Good Reason" To Terminate.**

in opening statement, he can use his roadmap in closing to emphasize to the jury that he followed through on his promises. I use a slide like this:

As we discussed in *Rule 3: Be Credible*, keeping your promises goes a long way in establishing credibility with the jury. Therefore, in closing, the attorney should emphasize that he did everything he said he would during trial. The attorney can emphasize the fact that he followed through on his promises by presenting to the jury a slide entitled "We Have Proved." This slide should mirror the roadmap slide shown during opening statement.

• *Utilize a Flashcard Approach*

Flashcards are one of the most tried and true methods to memorize information. We used them in grade school to learn addition and subtraction; our children use them for the same reason; and I bet our parents used them in the exact same way. Flash cards have helped generations master basic arithmetic. How can we tap into this wonderful learning tool in the courtroom? The exact same way they have been used for generations. If you have important facts, events, or numbers, create a memorable flashcard for these essential facts and show them to jurors throughout trial.

During opening statement, introduce the jurors to the facts of the case as well as to the witnesses from whom they will hear. You saw the slide that introduced the three brothers. Isn't that essentially a flashcard? While showing slides of the witnesses' faces and names, we can tell the jurors what we anticipate each witness will contribute to our case. We might even create slides that include pictures of particular witnesses and beside each picture a quote of what the jury will hear the witnesses say during trial. We have seen one example of that, but let me show you another one that I used in closing. In this particular instance, I was concerned that the jurors would disagree about what was said. So this time, instead of typing the words in the slide, I literally took an image of the trial transcript and put it next to a picture of the witness. Here is what it looked like:

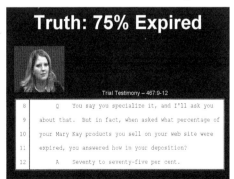

This flashcard shows a picture of the witness' face and her exact words. No one can argue with the transcript that I got directly from the court reporter. This also reinforces your credibility because you are not telling them what was said; you are showing them word-for-word what was said.

Using a flashcard approach with respect to expert testimony proves similarly valuable. I particularly like it with numbers. Here is a slide that I used in a recent closing. This particular expert was opining on the dollar value of damages to a building hit by a hail storm. It was the number that I was asking for in damages. I was a little worried because it was not a nice round number, making it harder to remember. So in closing I took a demonstrative that I had made during his testimony and placed it right next to his picture. Our expert was very knowledge-able, and the jury seemed to have liked him so I wanted to make sure they saw the number right next to his image before they went in the jury room. Here is the slide that I used in closing:

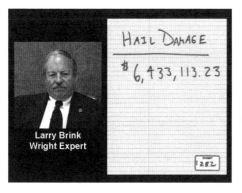

Right before delibera-tions, the jury saw the actual damage number we were seeking next to a photo of the very credible witness who suggested that number.

- ### *Use PowerPoint Slides to Wade through Documents*

PowerPoint slides can help direct the jurors' attention during witness examinations. They can also be helpful in guiding the jury through the evidence. During deliberations, we often take jurors out into a forest of evidence without providing them with any bread crumbs to find their way home. It is no wonder that jurors often feel lost in the midst of trial. Our job is to provide guidance to the jury. One method is to direct the jurors to particular trees of the evidence by converting documents important to the case into PowerPoint slides. One juror told us about an attorney who created a PowerPoint slide from a document crucial to the attorney's side of the case and then highlighted specific noteworthy portions of the document.

> *"A woman who was the witness and she had the paperwork/ documents. And they took the documents and put them on the screen—there was a screen—and highlighted some things. I guess it was some sort of PowerPoint because it came from his computer. Highlighted some things and asked her about different things. They had maybe two inches worth of documents that they had in front of them, and they didn't need to show us all two inches. They showed us parts that we needed, but certainly you got the idea that this is the whole record of the transactions between these people and here's what we found in this record. So we were able to listen to the witness tell us what the lines meant—what everything meant—and then see them for ourselves."*

Not only did this attorney point the jurors precisely to specific documents for later consideration during deliberations, but the attorney also directed them to exactly which sentences to pay attention to. Directing the jurors' attention is a much more effective method of trial presentation than briefly referencing important documents and then leaving it to the jurors to make of the documents what they will.

You can also use demonstratives to aggregate voluminous data. Remember the trial that I had for the executives who were terminated? To determine their damages, you had to sift through a lot of documents and a lot of numbers. I wanted to make the issue as easy for the jurors as possible. So I created a slide that summarized everything in one place, explained it, and totaled it. Here is the slide that we used:

Damages		
	Mr. Poss	**Mr. Green**
2008 Bonus	$437,634	$362,582
2009 Salary	$8,288	$6,794
Termination Benefit	$957,952	$793,765
Total	**$1,403,874**	**$1,163,141**

I took the damage number for each of these individuals and put it in one place. I also highlighted in red the most important numbers so there would be no doubt about what we were asking for in terms of a damage award.

• *Make Numbers Easy*

While we are on the subject of numbers, let's talk about more ways to make numbers accessible and memorable to jurors. Many people—not just lawyers—find numbers confusing and difficult. Juries are made up of people like you and me, so it is safe to assume that some of them have trouble with numbers as well. And if they do not have trouble with numbers, most find them boring.

When dealing with numbers, we run a high risk of boring and/or confusing the jury. This is especially the case when we must deal with multiple numbers during a single trial. Therefore, we must put the numbers in context and make the numbers as simple and as interesting as possible. It starts with the easy stuff. One juror expressed to us how helpful an attorney's highlighting the numbers in a PowerPoint presentation proved.

> *"The prosecutor for the bank had of course their PowerPoints—they were well put together. He had lots of places in the PowerPoint where he had highlighted things and it was eye-catching... That was kind of nice because you were dealing with numbers and it could be boring. That made it interesting."*

To make numbers as accessible as possible for the jurors, broach numbers in several different ways during trial. Using a variety of methods to address numbers including: (1) absolute numbers, (2) charts, (3) percentages, and (4) comparisons helps to prevent the jury from getting tripped up.

In a recent fraud case, the private placement memo at issue had promised investors a minimum of $5.8 million cash in the company at closing. Instead, at closing, the company had a mere $834,000. This was insufficient cash for the company, and the investors claimed that if we had known that is all the cash that would be present at closing we never would have invested. I was worried that this case would get confusing because of these two numbers, so we used several demonstratives to make the numbers more accessible. First, we used a slide that showed the amount that was promised compared to what was on hand at closing.

An excellent way to help jurors visualize how monetary sums compare to one another is by positioning one stack of bills next to another. Showing jurors the discrepancy between the two amounts really helped them to make sense of the numbers. This slide was used 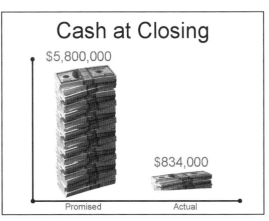 to contrast the difference between the amount promised and the actual amount received. We emphasized the comparison by explaining to the jury that at closing there was only 14% of the cash that was promised. We used the following slide to make that point:

In opening, with this slide as the background, I asked the jury to think about how upset they would be if their son or daughter brought home a 14 on their report card. Every juror understands that 14% is abject failure. Putting numbers in terms of percentages often has

a powerful effect on the jury because jurors encounter percentages in their everyday lives and easily understand them.

• *Fully Explain Damages*

One of the best ways to use PowerPoint presentations is in closing, especially with the jury questions. A lawyer once told me, "If you cannot say it to the jury, then the jury will never say it back to you." His point was that you have to tell the jury exactly what your client is asking them to do. In fact, without direction, there is no telling what the jury will award. To ensure that the jury knows exactly how to answer each question—whether it is yes or no or a dollar figure—you need to show them exactly how to complete the jury questions.

I literally scan each of the jury questions into PowerPoint slides, fill the numbers in and explain to the jury why we are asking them to make such an award. Here is a recent slide that I used in a closing:

You want to make sure the jury knows exactly what you are asking for so I write it down for them. I do the exact same thing if I am the plaintiff and asking for a damage award:

When I use these slides, I do not demand or instruct the jury to write these numbers down. Instead I tell them, "Based

QUESTION NO. 1:
EXISTENCE OF CONTRACT

Did the Defendants and Russell Alexander agree that Mr. Alexander would receive a one-third share of the profits in the Casas Del Sol Project in exchange for Mr. Alexander obtaining acceptable financing for infrastructure and construction for the Casas Del Sol Project?

INSTRUCTIONS

In deciding whether the parties reached an agreement, you may consider what they said and did in light of the surrounding circumstances, including any earlier course of dealing. You may not consider the parties' unexpressed thoughts or intentions.

An oral agreement bears the same force and effect in law as a written contract.

There is no agreement where the parties leave an essential term for later determination *and it is never determined.*

ANSWER Yes or No as to each of the following:

Texas Standard	**YES**
First LLD	**YES**
Ronald Dalton	**YES**

If you answered "Yes" as to any party in response to Question No. 3, then answer the following question. Otherwise, do not answer the following question.

QUESTION NO. 4:
CONTRACT DAMAGES

What sum of money, if any, if paid now in cash, would fairly and reasonably compensate Mr. Alexander for his damages, if any, that resulted from the Defendants' failure to comply?

INSTRUCTIONS

Consider the following elements of damages, if any, and none other:

1. One-third (1/3) of the profits in the Casas Del Sol Project earned in the past.

2. One-third (1/3) of the profits of the Casas Del Sol Project that, in reasonable probability, will be earned in the future.

Do not add any amount for interest on damages, if any.

ANSWER in dollars and cents.

Past 1/3 profits:	**$1,691,976.00**
Future 1/3 profits:	**$200,150.00**

on the evidence, we believe these are the correct numbers [or answers, as the case maybe]" and ask them to complete the jury questions in this way. The jury wants a specific reason for each dollar that it awards and does not like to feel that the attorney has arbitrarily selected numbers out of a hat. By carefully explaining what each number represents, the attorney ensures that the jury has a solid grasp on what amount of damages he is asking for and why he believes the facts of the case entitle his client to it. I usually add something like, "And if you are one of those people like me who has to write things down to remember them, this might be a good time to write them down." And I have to tell you that there is a whole lot of voodoo out there about what the jury will do, but I have never found anything better than watching to see how the jury reacts to my request to write things down. If they are writing, it looks good for the home team. If they just stare at you and write nothing down, you might think about rekindling your settlement negotiations.

As we discussed in *Rule 7: Get to the Point*, attorneys most effectively communicate with the jury when they use multi-sensory methods of teaching. When we accompany our statements to the jury with demonstratives, we engage both the jurors' auditory senses and their visual senses. By enabling the jurors to both hear and see the case, we facilitate the jurors truly learning the facts and arguments of our case so that they can use them during deliberations. We also enable the jurors to engage multiple senses simultaneously during trial by giving them the opportunity to take notes while watching the attorneys present the evidence. Prior to the commencement of the jury trial, the attorney should ask the judge for permission to provide the jurors with notepads on which they can take notes during trial. Jurors enjoy having something to do other than to simply listen to the attorneys and the witnesses for hours on end. One juror told us that note-taking helped him remain awake and attentive.

"I'm a note-taker—not because I refer to the notes later—but it helps me to concentrate and keep awake."

We are in favor of anything that keeps the jurors engaged and attentive.

Rule 10:
Present Credible Witnesses

We've spent a good bit of ink talking about the importance of a trial lawyer's credibility. In this chapter is an extension of that. It may not occur to you immediately, but the witnesses you present are an extension of your credibility. If you present good witnesses, it continues to reinforce the perception that you are a credible guide during the trial; a good lawyer would never present a witness who lacked credibility. On the other hand, if you present a witness who is not credible, for whatever reason, that too reflects on your credibility, but this time it is negative. In this chapter. We are going to look at various witness pitfalls through the eyes of the jurors. When you are preparing your witnesses for trial, and even deposition, keep these in mind as you work with your witnesses. It will be time well spent.

Jurors know people. They may not understand the details of a misdiagnosis of pancreatic cancer or the complications of a chemical formula for a patented product, but the one thing that all jurors have experience with is people. Now maybe they are good at evaluating people and maybe they are bad at evaluating people, but it is a safe bet that they think they have a lot more experience with people than the facts of your case. As a result, most jurors have definite opinions about when someone is being evasive, helpful, or indifferent. In fact, the more complicated the case is, the more important the people become. The less that a juror can access and understand the technical aspects of a case, the more they will rely on prior experiences and valuating people. This chapter is primarily about witnesses, but don't forget the central role that your credibility as the trial lawyer will play.

• *No One Likes an Evasive Politician or Witness*

When we asked jurors what makes a good witness, the most common response was that the best witness is one who answers the questions directly. Jurors like straightforward witnesses. Straightforward witnesses come across as far more credible than witnesses who, regardless of the questions asked, equivocate or pursue their own agendas in a partisan fashion.

How many times have we heard politicians and executives say "mistakes were made" instead of admitting they did something wrong. It is a complete shirking of responsibility because it places the blame out there somewhere on some unknown person or persons. It is a wholly unsatisfying response but has become the universal proxy for "we screwed up."

Everything I learned about bad witnesses, I learned from my children. Any of you who are or have been parents of young children know exactly what I am talking about:

> Father: (standing next to a broken vase and a
> child) Dear, how did this happen?
> Child: I was in my room playing with my
> dolls and I was dressing her in ski
> clothes.
> Father: Thank you for telling me that, but do
> you know how this happened?
> Child: Sissy came in my room and took the
> skis I was putting on Dolly.
> Father: What does that have to do with the
> broken vase?
> Child: You asked me what I was doing.
> Father: No, I asked you, "Do you know how
> this happened?"
> Child: I told you I was in my room.
> Father: Did you leave your room and
> come in this room?
> Child: Yes, but sissy ran away with my skis.

I could go on, but I am sure you get the picture. It may take me another half dozen questions, but you already know that this story will end with two little girls tearing through the living room and one of them hitting the vase, knocking it to the floor, and shattering it. In our experience, bad witnesses are very similar to children. They struggle mightily to evade tough questions. Just as this kind of questioning is difficult and frustrating to parents around the world, it is the same for jurors.

More importantly, evasiveness also sends a signal that a witness is untrustworthy. And here's what a juror said.

> *"A good witness presents evidence or presents a good picture of the scene or whatever as he sees it rather than evasiveness or rather than simply probably trying to stretch the truth more or less. If I see... a witness who is agitated along with being evasive, then he has, in my opinion, less credibility."*

Another juror spoke negatively of witnesses who couldn't get to the point during cross examination but who "danced around" instead.

> *"Witnesses obviously look bad when they were asked questions that they couldn't answer. And you could tell when they would get to the point; they would kind of dance around the question."*

Our witnesses, like the child in our example, fool no one and accomplish nothing when they equivocate and dodge. Once opposing counsel utters a question, the jurors want to know the answer. The jurors, experts on human behavior, know what a direct answer to a question sounds like. Jurors can therefore readily tell when a witness is avoiding an attorney's line of questioning. When a witness refuses to respond and forces the attorney to repeat his question in several different ways, the jury grows agitated. From the jurors' perspective, nonresponsive witnesses simply waste their time.

The jury's purpose during trial is to ascertain the truth of each side's case. The jury reaches its fact-finding conclusions by separating the wheat of the evidence from the chaff. The jury must distinguish between relevant, important information and peripheral, non-essential facts; therefore, an evasive witness forces the jury to work a great deal harder than a witness who answers questions directly. The other risk with an evasive witness is that the jurors lose faith in a witness and tune out everything that witness has to say. We need to recognize that the jury will eventually get to the bottom of the evidence with or without our witnesses' cooperation. Jurors greatly appreciate helpful witnesses; therefore, make clear to your witnesses that it is their job to clearly and directly answer the questions—whether they think the answer is good or bad. As lawyers, it is our job to demonstrate how those answers—good or bad—should or should not affect the outcome of the case. If there is one lesson that you learn about teaching witnesses how to answer questions, this is the most important: answer the question directly.

In addition to ensuring that witnesses do not dodge questions because they don't like the answer, make sure that witnesses stick to the point. A witness's veering off into tangential information or answering the question they want to answer gives jurors more potentially irrelevant evidence through which they must wade to get to the meat of the case. One juror lauded a witness who stayed focused on the facts of the case and never deviated into his opinions.

"She was very good. She was very focused on the case itself. She didn't veer into any kind of opinions. She answered the questions and clarified the questions in the case from both sides."

• *Jurors Do Not Find Forgetful Witnesses Credible*

A witness's claiming to be oblivious about a fact the jurors believe the witness clearly knows hurts the witness's credibility. One juror told us about a series of witnesses who claimed to not remember signing particular documents even when the attorney showed the witnesses the signed documents. The juror found all of the witnesses disingenuous and wholly lacking in credibility.

"In this particular case, the witnesses were not good. They didn't remember events very well that they should have probably been able to remember. And as soon as it was pointed out to them in writing where they had signatures, then they didn't remember doing the signatures. Now whether that was the attorney's fault because the attorney didn't explain what they were signing or

---

> *whether that was basically trying not to remember in order to be able to do something, you couldn't tell. It just seemed like it was a very poor set of witnesses."*

We need to be especially cautious about allowing our witnesses to respond to a question with "I don't remember." We have seen a plaintiff's lawyer use video of repeated "I don't know" answers by an executive to devastating effect. Think about it. Here is an executive. He is a highly intelligent and highly placed employee in the company. We are now at trial, the day of reckoning at the end of a two-year case. And all this witness can say is "I don't know." Is that going to be credible? Is that going to demonstrate a company that cares about the result in the case? We think not. It sends a message that after two years we did not even take the time to learn how to answer to these questions. Jurors expect parties to the lawsuit to have their stories straight. One juror told us about a plaintiff who claimed he could not recollect the important facts of his case.

> *"The one that was trying to be awarded for the money, he went up there and he couldn't remember. He was changing his stories a lot. So that's what really caught my attention—that he couldn't even remember… and he didn't have his story straight."*

Many jurors simply do not believe witnesses who claim not to remember facts central to the case. One juror informed us that even if a great deal of time had passed, he still would not believe a witness who allegedly forgot what had happened to him.

> *"She might not have been telling the truth. To me, if something happened to you, you're not going to forget, you know, I don't care what length of time it is. Or her lawyer had a recording of it, and so they should have went back over it, you know, before they presented their case so she would know what was going on."*

Trial is like a test. Jurors know that you are supposed to study and be prepared for a trial. If you fail to prepare and it shows in your testimony, jurors tell us they will hold it against us.

• *The Jury Analyzes the Witnesses' Non-Verbal Cues*

We must advise our clients and witnesses of the fact that while they are on the witness stand, the jury not only listens to and dissects every sentence they utter but also scrutinizes their facial expressions, their tone of voice, and their body language. One juror told us that she judged a witness's truthfulness by how the witness moved his eyes while on the witness stand.

> *"And you could read them by their eyes really. You read them by their eyes. I would read a person by their eyes and their behavior and how they change their story."*

Again we see an example of a juror using what she brought into the courtroom—years of experience in dealing with people. Jurors are quite confident in their judgment of a witness's credibility, and they will use that judgment (right or wrong) in reaching their verdict. Another juror expressed that a witness's lack of apparent confidence hurt the witness's credibility in the eyes of the juror.

> *"Her in particular, she didn't—she wasn't very confident about her answers. She didn't—she seemed to have some gaps. And several times she said she didn't remember things. Also, there was the issue about the child in her car. There were a lot of those loose ends that were never tied together, so she as a witness wasn't terribly credible."*

Understandably, the witnesses will be nervous while being grilled on the stand. But this is really something on which we as attorneys must work with witnesses. In my practice, we actually put witnesses in a witness box in our mock trial room to help them get a feel for testifying. We put them through a mock cross-examination and direct so they will have experienced the event before trial. You never want to put a witness in the box cold with no common experience to draw on. As you work with your witnesses, watch them and do not hesitate to correct aspects of their presentation. We often encourage the witnesses to answer boldly and with confidence in order to avoid the jurors' mistaking a witness's timidity for disingenuousness. We want to be clear—we are not advocating you instruct them as to how to testify on substantive issues. Your goal is to help them with the process to insure that the evidence they present is done so in the clearest and most credible manner.

• *Jurors Prefer Respectful Witnesses*

There is a great series of books by a man named Ferol Sams. A recurring reference throughout one of the books is to people who were "raised right." In the context of this book, it means people who were raised in the South and taught to say, "yes ma'm" and "no, sir." It means that someone's parent took the time to teach him or her to have good manners. We need to remind our witnesses of the same things our parents taught us about dealing with others: be courteous and respectful, even to opposing counsel on cross-examination. Listen to what this juror says to understand why we advocate this approach.

"You know, it just doesn't come across well to jurors if [the witness] gets combative with the attorneys."

Think about your experiences in real life. What is your appraisal of someone who gets defensive? Do you believe a person who goes on the attack in the face of constructive criticism? No, we are looking for a person to be objective and evaluate the criticism. The same thing happens with witnesses. If they are attacked and they get defensive, the jury thinks that the witness is hiding something and the questioner is right. Although jurors do empathize with and relate more to witnesses than to attorneys, jurors still have an aversion to seeing anyone, even a cross-examiner, treated with disrespect.

• *Jurors Want Consistent Witnesses*

Jurors always look for inconsistencies in the witnesses' stories. Several jurors have informed us that a witness's telling one story or having a nice easy-going attitude when his own lawyer directs him and then an entirely different story or persona when opposing counsel cross-examines him causes the jurors to raise their eyebrows. One juror told us about a plaintiff who drastically changed his story when cross-examined by the defendant's attorney. The plaintiff's failing to maintain consistency throughout the trial caused the juror to doubt the truthfulness of all of the plaintiff's responses.

"The defendant himself actually seemed credible to me. The plaintiff—she had some inconsistencies in her testimony which, while they weren't necessarily material to the case or the decision, maybe would leave you in the back of your mind wondering about the truthfulness of all her responses."

There it is—the seeds of distrust. If someone is lying on this little thing, how can he or she be trusted on the big things? Another juror equated cross-examination to a lie detector test and disclosed to us that witnesses who withstood cross-examination without altering their stories impressed him.

"I think the thing that I think made a good witness or a credible witness is someone who can actually stand up to the cross examination with the same answers they had previously. It's just like taking a lie detector test—you can pass a lie detector test if you tell the truth. And most people don't realize that the truth is the thing that works for the jury, because just like the judge can tell when somebody's lying, most jurors can, too."

The logic behind this is simple. If he tells the same story on direct as on cross, the witness will earn the respect of the jury. If the jury respects a witness as credible they will be able to do two things. First, they can rely on this witness. Second, they use the fact that the witness withstood cross-examination to argue that this is the one witness in the whole trial who should be believed or that this witness should be believed over a witness who wavered. In other words, it gives the juror something to use to make his point in the jury room.

Yet another juror emphasized the importance of a witness not wavering on cross-examination. The witness told us that a witness's consistent demeanor impressed him even when the witness answer was occasionally "I don't know."

> *"And so when the person was answering very directly and didn't waver, or on the other side, didn't know and admitted they didn't know, that can be very favorable."*

A witness's consistently telling the same story bolsters his credibility with the jury. On the other hand, the jury, quite rightly, finds an inconsistent witness, who contradicts himself, unreliable and untrustworthy. Believe us, witness credibility is exactly what drives and determines how the jury answers the jury verdict.

• *The Witnesses' Stories Need to be Believable*

Jurors understand that to some extent presenting a trial is like producing a play. This does not mean that a trial is make-believe. It means produce a play that has been reduced to its truthful essentials. The lawyers job is to focus the questions on the most essential events and the witness' job is to tell the truth about those events. We need to teach our witnesses to give natural responses without affectation. The vast majority of witnesses are not trained actors; therefore, the jury sees straight through a witness's endeavors to fake emotions. When it becomes obvious to the jurors that the witness's emotions and answers are not wholly genuine, the jury doubts the truthfulness of what the witness has to say. One juror told us that she doubted the testimony of a witness who responded to an attorney's inquiries in an overly emotional, clearly phony fashion.

> *"The plaintiff—there was what I saw to be very, very overly emotional, crying and things. I could tell this was not sincere— it was timed. And most of us had seen enough T.V. to know this is not going to have an effect. Although in our case, there were one or two of the jury members who were affected by the crying, and it was almost a negative effect."*

On this one, I go back to my example of the broken vase. What if the child's response to the question of what happened was to burst into tears? Do you think that means the child had no idea about what happened, or that the child is guilty and afraid of being punished, so she breaks into tears?

Another juror had similar thoughts on how a witness manufacturing emotion on the witness stand diminished the witness's credibility. This juror told us that she simply did not believe witnesses who put on exaggerated performances.

> *"[The witness] was not believable. Although I think she probably felt strongly about whatever it was, it was not believable. And there were just too many things that [seemed] put on. Her demeanor—oh, whoa is me! It was just a little too much."*

The larger point here is that emotion is a powerful force in the courtroom. If used appropriately, it can be effective; but when it is manufactured or put on, the jurors see it for what it was. Encourage your witnesses to be themselves when they testify. There is no need to reach for emotion or try to make something more than it is.

In addition to ensuring that the witness acts genuinely on the witness stand as opposed to putting on a performance, make sure that the witness's story makes logical sense. One incredibly insightful juror told us about her misgivings concerning a plaintiff who stated on the witness stand that she had severe back injuries, shortly after walking to the stand in three-inch heels.

"I don't know if she was making it up or just kind of making it sound worse than it was. And one thing—and this is maybe something really silly—but she was claiming all these back injuries and she couldn't run any more, and she was wearing three-inch heels in the jury room. Really, your back hurt so bad and you have those heels on—it made us wonder how bad is that back injury? Because I can't wear three-inch heels."

We have to tell you that as men, we probably would not have seen this had it been one of our trials. But it stands as a reminder that jurors are wicked smart. They read the witnesses down to most specific detail, including their shoes. We need to remember that jurors are often quite perceptive and are always full of common sense. Jurors never fail to pick up on minute details that cause a party's story to contradict logic.

• *Prepare Your Witnesses*

We mentioned the similarities between a trial and a test. Trial is the day of reckoning. It is a day that all disputes will be fully and finally resolved. When facing a test like that, is it normal to prepare? In our opinion, it is not only normal but it is required. Brooks Robinson famously said in reference to preparation, "If your're not practicing, somebody else is, somewhere, and he'll be ready to take your job." If you want to fail at trial, there is no better way than to fail to prepare your witnesses. Many lawyers worry that preparing a witness will make a witness seem rehearsed. Our response is that it depends on how you do it. If you give the witness a script complete with questions and answer, then yes you may end up looking rehearsed. But if you instead sit down with your witness without a script and run them through a series of questions on direct and cross, the witness will not look rehearsed. The witness will be prepared. And if you do not believe us, listen to what this juror told us about an obviously unprepared witness.

"The main plaintiff—now that it's coming back to me—did not seem like they had rehearsed. It didn't go well."

It is essential that we prepare our witnesses. Again, we want to emphasize that we are not telling you to woodshed witnesses and tell them what to say substantively. That would be unethical. But it is our job to put our best case forward. That means go through questions with the witness and if you are going to use exhibits, then include exhibits in the preparation. If the witness has never been run through a mock examination, the best case is a nervous witness and the worst case is you have prepared that witness to fail. We must prepare our witnesses not only for the direct examination but also for the questions opposing counsel will likely ask on cross. When we fail to prepare our witnesses in advance of trial, our witnesses come across as poorly prepared and rather incompetent to the jurors. The jury expects for both sides of the trial to have planned well so that the trial runs smoothly. When the attorney and his witnesses fumble around, it appears to the jury that the attorney and his side are not ready for the case.

• *Carefully Prepare Your Direct and Cross-Examinations*

Whether the jury finds a particular witness credible depends in part on which questions we choose to ask. We need to maintain control of our witness examinations. We must spend a great deal of time devising and organizing our questions so that we can most effectively direct our witnesses and cross-examine opposing counsel's witnesses. When preparing our direct examinations, we need to sequence our questions so that the questions and answers tell a logical story. When we jump from one topic to another, it makes it difficult for the jury to follow the witness's train of thought. Additionally, failing to lead our witnesses well and question them thoroughly creates gaps in the witnesses' stories. As we discussed previously in *Rule 6: Be Transparent*, jurors interpret gaps as the attorney's or the client's endeavoring to hide important evidence from them. The attorney needs to address the thorns in the witness's testimony when directing the witness. When the attorney fails to address potential problems with his witness's testimony on direct, he gives opposing counsel the opportunity to point out the glaring omissions on cross. A witness's coming across as inconsistent proves incredibly detrimental to the witness's credibility.

About the Authors

James M. Stanton assists businesses at all stages of litigation in federal and state court. Whether in the courtroom or at the settlement table, his experience as a state district judge and a board certified trial attorney helps his clients resolve their lawsuits so they can get back to focusing on their businesses. James joined Andrews Kurth following his service as presiding judge of the 134th Judicial District Court in Dallas County, Texas. During his career as a lawyer and judge, his experience includes handling over sixty jury trials, forty bench trials, and thousands of hearings. He is board certified in Civil Trial Law by the Texas Board of Legal Specialization.

Trey Cox specializes in courtroom fights between businesses. His jury trial experience and courtroom success have earned him the distinction of being Board Certified as a Trial Advocate by the National Board of Trial Advocacy. Trey represents Fortune 500 corporations, entrepreneurs, and leading firms in a wide array of industries. His dedication to his clients and winning track record have repeatedly earned him recognition as one of the top trial lawyers in the country.